Sketches
from the
Five States
of Texas

A Wardlaw Book

Sketches from the
Five States of Texas

A.C. GREENE

Texas A&M University Press
COLLEGE STATION

The paper used in this book meets the minimum requirements
of the American National Standard for Permanence
of Paper for Printed Library Materials, z39.48-1984.
Binding materials have been chosen for durability.

Library of Congress Cataloging-in-Publication Data

Greene, A. C., 1923–
        Sketches from the five states of Texas / A.C. Greene. — 1st ed.
            p.   cm. — (A Wardlaw book)
        Includes index.
        ISBN 0-89096-842-X (alk. paper). — ISBN 0-89096-853-5
(pbk. : alk. paper)
        1. Texas — History — Miscellanea.   I. Title.   II. Series.
F386.6.G74   1998
976.4 — dc21   98-22743
                                                                                    CIP

Most of these "Texas Sketches" in their original form
appeared in the *Dallas Mourning News.*

For Judy,

tender wife & tough critic

Contents

THE STATE OF CENTRAL TEXAS

Acknowledgments

I wish to thank all the readers of "Texas Sketches" who,
through the years, generously supplied so many topics
and made valuable additional comments to that column.
I have tried to give credit to these historical helpers
when their contributions
are used in this book.

A.C.G.

Publisher's Acknowledgment

The Texas A&M University Press is privileged to add its imprint to this Wardlaw Book. The designation claims a special place in the list of Texas A&M publications.

Supported with funds inspired by the initiative of Chester Kerr, former head of Yale University Press, this book, along with its companion volumes, perpetuates the association of Frank H. Wardlaw's name with a select group of titles appropriate to his reputation as man of letters, distinguished publisher, and founder of three university presses.

Donors of these funds represent a wide cross-section of Frank Wardlaw's admirers, including colleagues from scholarly presses throughout the country as well as those from other callings who recognize and applaud the many contributions that he has made to scholarship, literature, and publishing in his four decades of active service.

The Texas A&M University Press acknowledges with profound appreciation these donors.

Mr. Herbert S. Bailey, Jr.	John and Sara Lindsey
Mr. Robert Barnes	Mrs. S. M. McAshan, Jr.
Mr. W. Walker Cowen	Mr. Kenneth E. Montague
Mr. Robert S. Davis	Mr. Edward J. Mosher
Mr. John Ervin, Jr.	Mrs. Florence Rosengren
Mr. William D. Fitch	Mr. Jack Schulman
Mr. August Frugé	Mr. C. B. Smith
Mr. David H. Gilbert	Mr. Richard A. Smith
Mr. Kenneth Johnson	Mr. Stanley Sommers
Mr. Chester Kerr	Dr. Frank E. Vandiver
Mr. Robert T. King	Ms. Maud E. Wilcox
Mr. Carl C. Krueger, Jr.	Mr. John Williams
Mr. John H. Kyle	

Their bounty has assured that Wardlaw Books will be a special source of instruction and entertainment to the reading public for many years to come.

The Five States of Texas

Texas, through its annexation treaty with the United States in 1845, has a unique privilege. By the terms of that document, Texas has the right voluntarily to divide itself into five separate and independent states; it is the only one among the present fifty states with this designated ability. Historians don't seem to agree on why this provision was added to the annexation treaty. Perhaps, as some believe, it was inserted by a pro–slavery group who hoped that some day the slave states could increase voting power with such a split. Others believe that disgruntled elements within the Republic of Texas were determined to have their own political domain.

Political reasons aside, the State of Texas falls naturally into five geographically distinct "states"—East Texas, South Texas, North Texas, Central Texas, and West Texas—and the sections usually are viewed that way by Texas residents. You see or hear references made to the five states everyday in print, on the air, or in conversation: "Dottie is visiting her sister in East Texas," or "We went to South Texas on our vacation." Major city telephone directories include dozens of governmental organizations or private businesses with the regional designation in their names.

Bear in mind that, to a Texan, each of these place names carries with it a vision of climate, natural beauty (or lack of it), certain vagaries of weather, and other drawbacks or virtues, not only of the land but also of the people who live there. The Texan is fiercely proud of his locality, and if he cannot find anything good in it to brag about, he will brag about how bad it is. The land so often shapes the Texan that, to explain himself, he must defend it. Therefore, do not expect him to "understand" that some other place is better. "Don't ask a person where he is from," runs a folk proverb. "If he's from Texas, he'll tell you. Otherwise you'll embarrass him."

These, then, are sketches from the five states of Texas, with a few sections to begin with that involve the entire state. Some of the "five states" overlap, of course, because there are no fixed boundaries to these five states. Some of the implied boundaries are historical, some economic or cultural; some are emotional. These sketches are history-within-history, small biographies. Most of them give certain asides, certain views, certain comments on Texas life that are not generally known or not generally found together. They ordinarily represent something that we in

Texas think of as being peculiarly "Texan." Sometimes it's determination (which can become stubbornness), sometimes it's foolishness. Not all the heroes of Texas were heroic; there are cruel, unnecessary chapters of Texas history.

Today the denomination "Five States of Texas" has become something of a misnomer, although the five names are used hundreds of times every day. But today there are other "states" that could stand alone, particularly the Gulf Coast region, which includes Houston and Galveston; the land West of the Pecos; and the Panhandle. Each of the five states has one or two areas within its bounds that carry individual significance.

Another form of a state-within-a-state is found in Texas literature. The separate literatures of the various parts of Texas probably are as strong in their diversity as any other element among the five states. Little towns scattered across the face of Texas, such as Wharton, Trinity, Cumby, and Archer City, have contributed major writers, not just to their home state but to the world. Texas literature plays out differences in social and cultural approaches to history or to life within the varied regions. And most of the better writing in Texas has been done from the regional standpoint.

Is the history of Texas or of the Texans—the stories of the things they did, or things that happened to them—is this history different from all other histories, all other happenings in all other states? Yes and no. Unquestionably, much of the same thing occurs anytime humans are grouped together. But passing the boundaries of Texas, whether coming in from the East across the Sabine River, from the North across the Red River, or from the West or South across the Rio Grande, life seems to take on a different tinge, a different tone, once "Texas" is reached. "Movin' fu'ther west!" came to represent a Texan's freedom from impositions and rules; in the immense expanse of Texas, this freedom could be grasped without having to leave her borders. This is because Texas has another priceless inheritance from the time of the annexation treaty: it owns its own public lands. Even the federal government has to buy that land if it seeks to own some part of Texas.

All this comes together to form the diverse human and natural landscape of the Lone Star State. But, while each section may consider itself a separate country, not a one would sever its relations—political, economic, historical, social, or cultural—with the other four. As the late Texas author and storyteller, J. Frank Dobie, once wrote, Texas could never divide itself into five states or even two or three states: who would get the Alamo?

DIVIDING UP TEXAS

Even before annexation to the United States, the size of Texas drew fire. Sen. Thomas Hart Benton, of Missouri, proposed that Texas be reduced in size so that, if admitted, her area would not exceed that of the largest state then in the Union— which, not surprisingly, was Missouri. Congressman J. P. Hale of New Hampshire made the first proposal to divide Texas after it was admitted as a state. He proposed splitting Texas in two, drawing a line from the northwest corner of the Panhandle southeast to the Gulf of Mexico. West Texas, under his proposal, would be free, East Texas slave.

Isaac Van Zandt, the Republic of Texas minister at Washington during annexation negotiations, favored division, later making it his chief plank as candidate for governor in 1847. He died before the election was held. Senator Benton in 1850 again tried to reduce Texas's size, with a bill which would have made the Big Bend area and the northern Panhandle U.S. territory, the remainder of Texas to be divided into two states. Mississippi's Sen. Henry S. Foote (author of *Texas and the Texans,* published in 1841) countered with a proposal to make the territory east of the Brazos River and the 100th meridian into the "State of San Jacinto." In 1852, Texas legislator James W. Flanagan of Rusk would have divided Texas into two states by running a line up the Brazos to meridian 101.5 north. This was voted down 33 to 15.

Division sentiment was strong during the Reconstruction Convention of 1866. Three different plans would have split off the Trans-Pecos region, or separated Texas east of the Trinity River, or made a mostly German state in Southwest Texas. In 1868, Gov. Elisha Pease proposed to sell to the U.S. the territory west of a line drawn from the mouth of the Pecos northward.

That same year, a bill called "Congressional Plan of Reconstruction" was introduced in Congress to make three states: East Texas, to lie east of the Trinity; South Texas, to be a wide region bounded by East Texas and the Colorado River on the west; and the remaining state to be plain old Texas.

Texas Gov. E. J. Hamilton proposed a three-part division, with everything north of the 32nd parallel to be North Texas, the region south of the 32nd and east of the Brazos River to be East Texas, and the area south of the 32nd parallel and west of the Brazos to be West Texas. San Antonio was to be the capital of West Texas. Things went so far that a constitution for the State of West Texas was drawn up and printed (rare copies of that document today bring hundreds of dollars).

In 1869, a bill would have divided Texas into a state south and west of the Colorado River, to be named "State of Lincoln." In 1871, the final serious division attempt would have split Texas into four states, roughly matching the four directions, with West Texas, the largest, embracing modern western Texas and the Panhandle.

Sketches
from the
Fives States
of Texas

The
One
State
of Texas

TEXAS RIVER NAMES

Every part of Texas is crossed by two or three major rivers, a good many of them rising within the state. Texas rivers are celebrated in countless stories and songs, many in Spanish as well as English. Which is appropriate, since the major rivers of Texas were named by the Spanish explorers. The Red River (Rio Roho, among other names) was discovered and may have been named as far back as Coronado's 1541 expedition, and certainly it was called by that "Red" name by the seventeenth century.

The Sabine River, which forms a long portion of Texas' border with Louisiana, had a tumultuous record during the years when it was the controversial boundary between, on the one hand, the United States and, on the other, the Spanish, then the Mexican province of Tejas, then the Republic of Texas. The effects of the Neutral Zone, established between the Republic and the U.S., lasted into Texas statehood and encouraged criminals and crime even after the bounds of statehood were settled. The Sabine was named early in the eighteenth century; the name designates cypress trees—as does Sabinal, the name of a river in Uvalde County. There is a mysterious note concerning Sabine Lake, which is formed near the coast at the confluence of the Sabine with another Spanish-named river, the Neches. There a seventeenth-century Spanish priest, led by Caddo Indians, was shown the wrecked hull of an English ship loaded with brick—surely the most "off-course" ship in Texas history, as there were no English settlements nearer than the Atlantic Coast.

Because much of the Texas soil through which rivers flowed was reddish in color, a second "red" river was the Colorado of Texas. The name is ironic, however, because it is one of the few rivers flowing out of West Texas that is mainly clear and clean. Most geographers believe that *Colorado* originally was applied to the Brazos. The Spanish name for the Brazos, Rio de los Brazos de Dios ("River of the Arms of God"), has puzzled researchers for centuries and has given rise to folk tales of how Spanish expeditions were saved by a parting of the waters or a sudden flood which destroyed their enemies. However, no evidence has been found in any Spanish archive for this basis of the name.

Confusion also exists over the Trinity River's name. In its upper reaches, three forks flowing together create the main stream. An early designation for the modern Dallas area was "The Three Forks." Many people feel the tripartite name, Trinity, is of this natural origin. However, the river was named "Trinity" some three hundred river miles downstream, and many decades before the historic name "Three Forks" was in use. Alonso de León, who named the river, had no idea that there were three forks to the stream farther north. He named it Holy Trinity ("la Santísima Trinidad"), possibly because it was Trinity Sunday when he named it.

Most of the rivers of Texas, head up in Texas. Two do not: the Rio Grande ("Rio Bravo del Norte" of the Spanish) starts in Colorado, and the Pecos begins in New Mexico. The Canadian, which crosses the Texas Panhandle, also rises in Colorado. (The origin of the name *Canadian* is uncertain; does it come from the Spanish, meaning "canyons," or is it named for a French-Canadian party of the eighteenth century?)

"Nueces" is probably the oldest river name in Texas, coming from "the river of nuts" described by Cabeza de Vaca in the 1530s. Some modern historians, however, think the river Cabeza de Vaca described was more likely the Guadalupe. Cabeza had been captured by an Indian tribe on the Texas Gulf Coast and visited his "river of nuts" with his captors during harvest season.

Some historically important smaller rivers, such as the Clear Fork of the Brazos in West Texas (which isn't very clear), the Devils River in the Trans-Pecos area, and the Clear Fork of the Trinity (Tarrant County), were named by later settlers. The Devils River, which empties into Lake Amistad, is said to have been given that name by Col. Jack Hays. When he was told it was "Saint Peter's River," he stared into the dark, gloomy canyons through which it runs and stated, "Looks more like the devil's river to me."

The Spanish made some mistakes, too. Salado (Salty) Creek, in Bell County, is spring fed and was wondrously clear, with nary a drop of salt.

COUNTY ODDITIES

Texas has 254 counties named for an astonishing variety of people and things. Among them: Texas heroes, Mexican heroes, U.S. heroes, and Confederate heroes—but not Jeff Davis as president of the Confederacy. Jeff Davis County was named for Jeff Davis as U.S. Secretary of War, 1853–57. Texas counties are also named for lilies, rivers, editors, poetics, Indians, presidents, preachers, geological formations, doctors, Greek letters, trees, reporters, saints, angels, Alamo victims, inventors, and Spanish, Mexican, and French notables, including the Marquis de Lafayette.

An equally astonishing number of counties and cities with the same name are not associated with one another. Austin, the state capital, is not in Austin County, Houston is not in Houston County, Taylor is not in Taylor County, Tyler is not in Tyler County, and Rusk is not in Rusk County. The list goes on: the cities and towns of Cameron, Crockett, Bowie, Henderson, Kenedy, Kleberg, Pecos, Sherman, Terrell, and Yoakum are not located in similarly named counties.

Certain cities should be in certain counties, one would think, but they aren't. Colorado City is not in Colorado County. Robert Lee is not in Lee County, although both city and county are named for Gen. Robert E. Lee. Johnson City is not in Johnson County, Castroville not in Castro County (both are named for French colonizer Henri Castro). De Leon, the town, is not in Leon County, Smithville is not in Smith, Stephenville not in Stephens, and Gainesville not in Gaines. Caldwell is not in Caldwell County but is the county seat of Burleson County; but the town of Burleson isn't located there. Neither Woodsboro nor Woodville is in Wood County (nor is Oakwood). Jacksonville is in neither Jack nor Jackson counties, and neither Kingsville nor the King Ranch is in King County. Jefferson is not in Jefferson County or Jeff Davis County, and neither Greenville nor Tomball is in Tom Green County.

Some natural associations could be made. Sugar Land and Sugar Hill should be in Loving County, but aren't. (Neither is much else. Loving is the least populated county in the state.) Down along the Gulf Coast is Jackson County, where Edna, Lolita, Olivia, and Francitas dwell—and they could be from the Vanderbilt, the Morales, or the LaSalle families, all of whom also dwell in Jackson County.

Anson is county seat of Jones, named for Anson Jones, last president of the Republic of Texas, Gail is the county seat of Borden, named for dairyman Gail Borden, and Emory is county seat of Rains, named for Emory Rains of the Republic. Collin McKinney's name got twisted. The county is Collin, and its seat is McKinney. And Texas County isn't in Texas; it's in Oklahoma.

RAIL NICKNAMES

Texans bestowed all kinds of nicknames on their railroads—out of affection, frustration, or peculiar circumstances. A few became official, like Katy for the former

Missouri-Kansas-Texas Railway; or MoPac for the Missouri-Pacific. Here are some of the better remembered Texas rail nicknames. "Hell Either Way Taken" was the Houston East & West Texas, a narrow-gauge road now part of the Southern Pacific system. "Wobblety, Bobblety, Turnover & Stop" (also: "Won't Be Back Till Saturday") was the Waco, Brazos, Trinity & Sabine. "Quit Achin' & Push" meant Quanah, Acme & Pacific. The Trinity & Brazos Valley was "Try & Be Virtuous"—also called "The Boll Weevil," because it crept across the Blacklands cotton country. "Aged & Slow" designated the late Abilene & Southern.

"Ever Late & Rarely Runs" was the East Line & Red River, also known as "Everlasting Rail Road." The former Texas & Pacific was called "Time & Patience." "Descend & Walk" was given the Dallas & Wichita (which became the Denton branch of the old Katy). "Misery & Eternal Torment" honored the Marshall & East Texas line. "The Saap" was the affectionate title for the San Antonio & Aransas Pass. "Mule Power" (also "The Mop Line") was the Missouri-Pacific. "The Sausage Line" denoted the San Antonio, Uvalde & Gulf (SAU&G). "The Gospel Road" marked the Bartlett & Western, because of sidings named Matthew, Mark, Luke, and John. (It also was called "The Bull Frog" because it connected Bartlett and Florence.) "Got Tired and Walked" referred to Gulf, Texas & Western.

"Whiskey, More Whiskey & No Water" was hung on the Weatherford, Mineral Wells & Northwestern. "The Pa & Ma" was the Paris & Mount Pleasant. "Tin Can Railroad" was the old Texas Central. A surviving segment at Gorman is "The Peanut Line," because that's its cargo. "The Circus Line," the Eastland, Wichita Falls & Gulf, was called that because it was built with Ringling Brothers Circus money. "The Soup Line" (also "SOP"): Southern Pacific. "Till Mañana": Texas-Mexican Railroad.

F. L. Stead of Dallas reports that his favorite was the Corpus Christi, San Diego and Rio Grande Narrow Gauge Railroad; it had the longest name of any railroad built in Texas, and the longest nickname, too: "Confounded Contraption, Somewhat Dilapidated, Runs Good, Needs Grease." (Mr. Stead grew up in northern Ohio, where the Wheeling & Lake Erie was "Walk & Leave Early.") Ray Peeler, Jr., of Bonham tells of the Denison, Bonham & New Orleans, or "Dead Broke & Not Operating." Mrs. M. J. Canterbury of Kilgore recalls that, when she was a young passenger, she heard a conductor on the Missouri & North Arkansas line call it "May Never Arrive." She noted, "I was very relieved to learn he spoke in jest."

From a Waco reader comes this nickname: "Runs Slow & Peculiar" for the Roscoe, Snyder & Pacific. John B. McCall of Coppell—whose stationery is colorfully decorated with steam railroad scenes—contributes "Rushup & Push" for the RS&P.

"Always Talking Safety First," for the Atchison, Topeka & Santa Fe, was more than just a nickname. It became the company's slogan in the early 1920s. The Santa Fe even published a song, "Rally 'Round the Safety Habit," with words by J. D. M. Hamilton, claims attorney for the Santa Fe system. Hamilton's words proclaimed: "Shouting the battle cry of Safety, we'll rally from our shops, and we'll rally from our trains. . . . Down with carelessness, and up with more care." (The tune was "Rally 'Round the Flag, Boys.")

Lefty Creekmore, of Dallas, says that, when he was a boy in Jermyn, out in Jack County, the main attraction for the townspeople (as in dozens of other small Texas towns) was gathering at the depot to greet the 4 P.M. arrival of the Gulf, Texas & Western, which he called "Getcha Ticket & Walk" or "Galvanized Tanks & Windmills." He adds, "After the train pulled out, everyone would follow the old fellow that picked up the mailbag and took it to the post office. Everyone hung around until advised that all the mail had been sorted. You checked your box to see if you had received any mail, then it was time to go home."

OLD HIGHWAY
DAYS AND WAYS

Back when the best Texas paving was brick—or gravel—driving an automobile was an adventure and could be hazardous. For example, the highway between Van Alstyne and Sherman, in North Texas, was merely two runners of pavement with a turnout here and there so that cars could pass. There were rules of the road as to which car had to back up on single-lane highways with "pullouts." Arm signals persisted past World War II: the left hand, down at a forty-five-degree angle, meant "slow" or "stop"; up in a right angle meant "right turn"; straight out was "left turn." (Lighted turn indicators and air-conditioning did away with hand signals.) Even in the 1930s, there were skips in the pavement, called "holidays," where sections of road were left unpaved because the adjoining landowner refused to pay for his portion. (Farmers complained that motorists, needing a lever to get out of the mud, would tear down a fence to obtain a post.) And for twenty years, all "V-8s" were Fords.

Until the middle twenties, gasoline was a problem. Not only were filling stations sometimes many miles apart, but their storage tanks weren't always waterproof. Some gasoline had to be strained through chamois to remove impurities such as water.

But the real automotive hex was tires. To get two thousand miles from a tire was remarkable, and few motorists taking a trip of more than a hundred miles did not have to change at least one flat. Tire troubles involved words and phrases motorists of today have never known, or have forgotten: "breaking a rim," "inserting a boot," hot patch versus cold patch, regrooving. All kinds of tires, from bicycles to automobiles, had inner tubes.

Side curtains had isinglass inserts that gradually turned brown and checkered. There was a hole on the driver's side so that he, or she, could stick out an arm and give hand signals. Mud, of course, was a constant enemy, and many a farmer was called out with his team to extract a stuck automobile. In fact, some were called "mud farmers," because, it was claimed, they kept a mudhole on the nearby dirt road full of liquid—while they stood by with a team of mules, charging as much as five dollars, a day's salary, to pull you out.

The Lone Star State had its share of homemade automobiles. Many, if not most, of the names have been forgotten. Texas got its first automobile in 1899, but the horseless carriage caught on quickly in Texas. Houston, in 1905, had only eighty cars, but by 1911 the city had over one thousand automobiles.

In Houston in 1905, Southern Motor Car Company began marketing the "Dixie," assembled from parts shipped in. The company failed after producing seventeen automobiles. In 1920, the Southern Motors Manufacturing Association, Ltd., offered the "Ranger Four," a five-passenger, four-cylinder model which claimed it could travel fifty miles per hour without vibrations. The company went into receivership in 1922.

In 1911, an Arlington factory built the Little Kar (named for the factory owner, not for its size), and at about the same time a Cleburne factory was turning out the Luck Utility. In fact, Cleburne produced several makes: in 1913, the Cleburne and a model called the Chaparral. From 1918 until 1922, the Texan and the Texan truck were built at Cleburne and Fort Worth. In Grand Prairie, the Little Motor Kar Company built a delightful vehicle named the Texmobile, while the Texas Truck and Tractor Company made the Texas truck in 1920. Fort Worth also saw the Bridges automobile in 1918 and the McGill in 1922. The Lone Star Motor Company of San Antonio for a brief while (four years) made the Lone Star, and El Paso supposedly made another "Texas" motor car. (There were several proposed vehicles bearing the "Texas" marque. Whether they were ever made—that's a question.)

The Wichita Truck Company of Wichita Falls was the most successful motor enterprise in the state. The company built a complete line of vehicles, including heavy, chain-drive, off-road trucks much favored by the lumbering industry. Wichita trucks found a national market from 1911 until the Depression ended things in 1932. Someone tried the "Dallas" in 1931, and Fort Worth offered a quaint "Roadable" in 1946, built in Garland by Southern Aircraft. Unfortunately, few of Texas' cars were built and fewer were sold; the companies went through constant reorganization. Through the years, different firms operated the same factories. Hype was heavy: officers of one Dallas auto manufacturing firm were all arrested for fraud in 1920. The irony is that, if a few of their Texas autos were on hand today, they'd be worth a fortune.

EARLY TEXAS FILM INDUSTRY

Not surprisingly, given its year-round good weather and its colorful reputation, Texas was projected as a film center early in the history of the movie industry. Independent studios eventually operated, or at least were set up, across Texas, some producing pictures, some "film studios" in name only.

Movies first were shown commercially in Texas in 1897, but the first film reportedly shot in Texas was newsreel footage of the "Crash at Crush," a staged locomotive collision on the Katy Railroad in 1896. A newspaper reported that the footage would be made by "a man from New York" using a "kinetescope" [sic], probably one of Thomas Edison's Kinetoscope machines. Another early film known to have been shot in Texas depicted the Galveston hurricane and was issued by the Edison Company three weeks after the September 1900 disaster. In 1908, a Danish film, *Texas Tex,* became the first to capitalize on the state's name, according to *Cowboys and Cadillacs,* Don Graham's book about Texas-related motion pictures.

Texas movie production began by 1909, when the Star Film Ranch started work in San Antonio. The Star Film Ranch was directed by Gaston Mèliés, brother of the famous French illusionist and cinematographer, Georges Mèliés. Star's first release was *Cyclone Pete's Matrimony* in 1910. Its last (1911) was *Immortal Alamo,* with Francis Ford, John Ford's older brother, as Davy Crockett.

In 1910, in Houston, Wesley H. Tilley and his brother Paul began making documentary-type footage ("U.S. Army's First Airplane"). Moving to San Antonio, they set up Satex Film Company, then transferred to Austin in 1913, producing six adventure films altogether. In 1910, King Vidor (1894–1982), who went on to be a famous Hollywood director, began making newsreels in his native Galveston. (The present-day town of Vidor was named for his father.) An overlooked early Texas movie maker ("manufacturer of all kinds of motion pictures") was E. H. Fitzhugh, who grew up in Dallas and for years was associated with theatrical management until returning to Dallas in 1910. According to a mug-book entry, he "began making films of picture-plays in various parts of the state . . . (then) animated cartoons." But Fitzhugh's importance lies in the fact that he began successful commercial, industrial, and educational specialty motion picture production, having "the only (studio) like it in Texas" by 1920.

Although Dallas, Houston, and Austin all were involved, San Antonio was the center of short-lived early Texas film making. Character actor and native son Maclyn Arbuckle, with the help of Will C. Hogg, organized the San Antonio Picture Corporation in 1918, producing "Maclyn Arbuckle Photo Plays."

Although no films from there have been found, Buffalo Gap, a beautiful village in southern Taylor County, attracted a movie maker, according to a business card of that period found by this writer. The card lists "Westex Pictures Company," with one Don I. Gray as the first manager.

The
State
of East
Texas

EAST TEXAS

East Texas is where much Texas history has entered Texas. The cities of Nacogdoches and San Augustine were among the first to attract Anglo settlers, well before Austin established his colony. Sam Houston settled first in San Augustine when he came to Texas from the Cherokee Nation. East Texas elicits some of the same conflicting feelings of fear and love that the West Texas landscape so often evokes. You sense, rather than know, when you are in East Texas, entering its deep forests, its piney woods, and such mysterious areas as shadowy Caddo Lake and the fabled Big Thicket.

East Texas is a land of water—rivers, huge lakes—and red and black lands. There are small towns off the highways, surviving on back roads, that have been there a hundred and fifty years. There are many places in East Texas where you can escape the notice of the world—or your neighbors. You can escape the world itself and be not so much out of date as out of the way; retire and hide, if you will. Nature, in East Texas, creates a paradise for certain kinds of hunters, fishers, outdoorsmen—and members of the human race with cranky notions, private views and pleasures. East Texas is full of people who have decided to leave the larger community and dwell in a smaller peace.

On the other hand, the legendary East Texas Oilfield is still the world's idea of sudden, unbelievable wealth—wealth that saw dirt farmers become millionaires before they could count that high. East Texas, going back to the early nineteenth century, has been the home of those furnaces that have produced the Texas iron and steel industry; and there are forgotten towns and sites where dreams of iron wealth once flourished—and where entrepreneurs tried to secure that wealth: places like New Birmingham, once proud, now forgotten. But where East Texas once was the world's largest cotton-producing area, cotton has moved to the West Texas Plains and the Panhandle, and East Texas has become the dairy center of the Southwest. The forests of East Texas, though now often plantations with pine trees growing in uniform rows, have supported a lumber industry for a century and a half, with tiny lumber railroads once reaching like many fingers into the depths and fastness of the Texas woodlands. And at one time or another, East Texas has led the nation in the production of tomatoes, black-eyed peas—and mules.

East Texas was southern. The largest plantations in Texas, and the most slaves, were in East Texas. East Texas was the setting for some of the worst blood feuds, and for political wars such as that between the Regulators and the Moderators. But East Texas has given the world astonishing quality in the arts: famous novelists, black musicians such as Leadbelly, actors and actresses of both races—and, almost as important, philanthropists.

East Texans generally are viewed by the rest of Texas as sharp, good salesmen, crafty in their business dealings—*cooney* is the old word, implying smart as 'coons and attuned to the nature of things. They are able to get the most out of an opportunity, whether in oil, law, or selling used cars. East Texas salesmen, some a generation or two away from the place, still operate all over the five states of Texas. With many of the region's native sons and daughters, be they world famous or wealthy as kings, East Texas never leaves their blood.

East Texas, like South Texas, is more self-contained than West or Central Texas; but East Texas, like most of the "five states," has imprecise boundaries. Beaumont, for example, is in Deep East Texas; but does East Texas include nearby Houston and Galveston? Palestine and Marshall unquestionably are in East Texas, but what about such edge towns as Calvert, Hearne, or College Station? Despite blurred edges to the west, the north, and the south, there are few other parts of Texas that can declare with such certainty, "I am where I am," and have everybody understand.

LOS ADAES

Settled by the Spanish in 1716, Los Adaes was the first colonial capital of Texas, although located in Louisiana. It served in that capacity from 1729 to 1773. (In fact, it would be 1836 before the capital of Texas actually was located in Texas.) The mission and presidio of Los Adaes was located east of the Sabine River in Louisiana, near present-day Robeline, south of Natchitoches.

The Domingo Ramón Expedition of 1716 founded the mission of San Miguel de Linares de los Adaes, and in 1721, the Aguayo Expedition set up the Presidio de Nuestra Señora del Pilar de los Adaes. The purpose was to stop French expansion into Texas, the border at the time not being well established. The French protested vigorously at having a military force so near Natchitoches (only fifteen miles), but in reality, both Los Adaes and the French town benefited greatly from the presence of the other, as contraband and international trade kept both alive at the time.

Los Adaes, named for a tribe of Caddoan Indians of the vicinity, prospered for fifty years, facing the French (whom the Spanish greatly feared) yet serving as diplomatic center for encounters between both countries. When France ceded Louisiana to Spain in 1762, Los Adaes was no longer important as a guard against French incursion, and in 1773 the inhabitants were ordered to move to San Antonio. However, several dissatisfied families under Gil Antonio Ybarbo, in April 1779, moved back east as far as Nacogdoches, which had been founded by Ramón in the same year as Los Adaes. Nacogdoches, attracting many Anglo adventurers, was a center for plots, intrigue, and actual warfare both well before and after the Texas Revolution.

The first European settlement in East Texas had been the Mission San Francisco de los Tejas, established in 1690 by Alonso de León near Weches in Houston County. It was abandoned in 1693. (Arguably, Ysleta and certain towns south of El Paso are the oldest inhabited settlements in Texas.)

ALONSO DE LEÓN NAMED TEXAS

A Mexican-born Spanish officer named most of the major Texas rivers—and named Texas itself. He was Alonso de León, born in 1640 in Cadereyta, Mexico (near Monterrey). In 1690, as governor of the Province of Coahuila, he led his fifth *entrada* (expedition) into what is now East Texas to found the first Spanish mission, San Francisco de los Tejas, among the Tejas (Hasinai) Indians in present-day Houston County. Thus this northeastern frontier of Spanish Mexico was provided with a name.

Earlier, during a fourth entrada, Captain de León named the Nueces River, the Hondo, the Medina, and, for himself, the Arroyo de León (now called the San Antonio River). He also named the Guadalupe, the Navidad (which he called San Marcos), the Colorado, and the Brazos de Dios (which he called Colorado). Historians think the latter names were confused: the Colorado ("red" in Spanish), where he crossed it, was a clear stream, while the Brazos more often was red. Captain de León named the Trinity (La Santisima Trinidad) without realizing that the river was formed by a trinity of upper branches, in an area (around modern Dallas) later called "The Three Forks."

Leon County was in Alonso De León's 1690 path, but its naming is uncertain; it could have been named for a legendary yellow wolf, called "león" or lion (unlikely), or for Martín de León, who founded Victoria (just as unlikely). The Leon River is said to have been named for Captain de León by the Aguayo Expedition of 1721. The Marquis de Aguayo, like Captain de León, was governor of Coahuila, and when the Aguayo Expedition crossed the Little River in Bell County, it may have done so where the León and the Lampasas come together to form the Little River. Or was the León in fierce flood and therefore called "león" or "lion"? In short, the captain's name may be on a number of Texas places but, ironically, none he named.

Up in Comanche County, citizens of De Leon, which is near the Leon River, say their town is named for Alonso, although Captain "Day-lay-OHN" might not recognize the honor if he heard it conferred. The town is universally referred to as "Dee-Lee-ahn."

CHAMP D'ASILE

A new Napoleonic empire in Texas? This seems to have been the underlying dream of a group of French refugees, including two of Bonaparte's generals, who came to Texas in 1818 to establish a colony called Champ d'Asile (Place of Asylum).

The leader was Charles Francois Antoine Lallemand, one of the emperor's "old guard." General Lallemand fled to the United States in 1816 and apparently quickly launched a scheme to establish a French military outpost in Spanish Texas which might help Joseph Bonaparte, Napoleon's brother and the deposed king of Spain (Joseph was in the United States), take Mexico and then rescue the emperor from Saint Helena and install him in North America.

Early in 1818, some 150 persons, under command of Gen. Antoine Rigaud, an older officer, reached Galveston Island, then the primitive headquarters of pirate Jean Lafitte, who also was French. After over two months, and (according to one account) as the first arrivals were on the point of cutting each other's throats, Lallemand appeared with more troops—including Spaniards, Poles, and Ameri-

cans—to make 400 colonists. Lafitte sold the group boats, and they rowed up the
Trinity River to a site about three miles north of Liberty. Here four forts and several log residences were built (contemporary drawings picture impossibly elaborate structures). Despite the presence of a few families, military order was observed,
and those same contemporary drawings show officers wearing their swords as other
colonists go to work sawing and hewing. But permission to settle on Spanish territory had been neither requested nor given, and Lallemand arrogantly had proclaimed to the Spanish court his intention to settle in Texas regardless. Within a
few weeks, the Spanish governor of Texas was ordered to send troops to Champ
d'Asile. Hearing of this, the French, who, having spent more time in military drill
and hunting than in agricultural pursuits, were by now near starvation, hastily
packed up and returned to Galveston. There they remained as unwanted guests
of privateer Lafitte, while Lallemand decamped to New Orleans, never to return
to Texas.

A hurricane, which put Galveston Island under five feet of water, caused several deaths and ruined any remaining goods the colonists had. Several colonists
departed overland for Louisiana; and in October, when Lafitte offered them use
of a captured ship, General Rigaud and most of the others sailed to New Orleans.
A few stayed at Galveston or went to Nacogdoches. Lallemand remained in
America until 1830, when he was allowed to return to France. A novel, *L'Heroine
du Texas,* and other French literary works, romanticized the bucolic colony, and
the military intent of Champ d'Asile generally was not understood until the twentieth century.

THE MYSTERY OF THE
YELLOW STONE

On March 31, 1836, when Gen. Sam Houston was leading his Texian army in a
"strategic withdrawal" in the face of Gen. Santa Anna's forces, he came to the
Brazos River, which was in flood, and learned that the steamboat *Yellow Stone* was
at Jared Groce's plantation, loading cotton. It had rained for four days, and the
wagons were bogging down, not to mention the soldiers. Meanwhile, Santa Anna,
having taken the colonial capital of San Felipe de Austin, was building and col-
lecting craft with which to ferry across the swollen Brazos. He felt certain that

Houston's army could not cross the river in time to impede his plan to capture President David Burnet and his cabinet, who were stranded at Harrisburg.

Houston decided that his best move was to descend the Brazos as quickly as possible, so as to surprise the Mexican forces. Therefore, on April 2, Houston "directed [the *Yellow Stone*] to be taken in charge for the use of the army." Piling bales of cotton around vital areas of the boat, Captain Ross announced that he was ready to transport five hundred men and baggage, and by April 13 everybody was across the river, with only one yoke of oxen lost. On April 14, Houston turned the *Yellow Stone* loose, and the boat steamed on downriver, running the gauntlet of Mexican fire. The *Yellow Stone* made it to Galveston, where Burnet and his cabinet finally had landed, and at the news of Houston's victory at San Jacinto, the *Yellow Stone* again was pressed into Texas service to haul the government officials. President Burnet, who hated Houston, refused to let the wounded victor aboard for a trip to New Orleans to seek medical aid, claiming that, with the revolution ended, Houston no longer was commander-in-chief and therefore was not entitled to government transportation. Captain Ross refused to leave without Houston, so, on the trip back from New Orleans to Galveston, the *Yellow Stone* carried the victorious Houston, President Burnet, and the Texas cabinet, as well as Gen. Santa Anna and forty-seven captured Mexican officers and soldiers.

The steamboat *Yellow Stone,* recognized immediately after San Jacinto for its role in Gen. Sam Houston's success at that battle, performed other important acts in Texas history.

In December 1836, it was the duty of the *Yellow Stone* to convey the body of Stephen F. Austin, the Father of Texas, to its burial place at Peach Point Plantation on the Brazos. Early in 1837, the boat brought Gail Borden, Dr. Francis Moore, and their press to the new capital of Houston, enabling them to found the first newspaper there, the *Telegraph and Texas Register.* A short time later, the boat deposited John James Audubon and his son, who were exploring the coastal bays of Texas, in the new city as guests of Old Sam. In June, the *Yellow Stone* billed the Texas Navy for towing one of its decrepit warships. Then it disappears from Texas history.

Known and loved, a legend in her own time, said by Houston to have "enabled me to save Texas," there is nothing to document her fate. (Originally built for service on the upper Missouri River, the name *Yellow Stone* honors the Yellowstone River.) True, legends persist that the boat was sunk in the Brazos or Buffalo Bayou, and a bell is displayed at the Alamo, said to be the *Yellow Stone's,* with the top portion shot, or snagged, away. Recent research has found mention of a *Yellow*

Stone's using a canal at Louisville, Kentucky, later in 1837. But is it the Texas *Yellow Stone*? If so, what happened to her?

Historian Donald Jackson, in his book, *Voyages of the Steamboat Yellow Stone* (from which much of this account is taken), likens her to the famous Flying Dutchman, doomed to roam the seas and never to make port. Jackson fantasizes, "She is trying to cross the bar at the mouth of the Brazos and the signal lantern's missing . . . she is a ghost ship."

PETER WHETSTONE

Before 1842, while the town of Pulaski was serving temporarily as the seat of Harrison County, there was great rivalry among landowners, each eager to have the permanent county seat located on or near his headright. Peter Whetstone, a member of the locating committee, seemed to offer the best location, but one member of the committee, John M. Clifton, refused to vote for it. After Whetstone had conducted a visit to his proposed location, Committeeman Clifton said, "Yes, the elevation is all right, the views are picturesque . . . but it is too dry, can't you see?"

Whetstone, without another word, reached into the hollow of a tree he happened to be leaning against, and brought out a demijohn which he handed to Clifton. The commissioner uncorked it, pulled heavily at the black bottle, and passed it on to the next man, who did likewise. When it got back to Whetstone, it was empty. Clifton at once withdrew his objection, admitting he had been mistaken about the land being too dry. Thus the new county seat, Marshall, was laid out on Whetstone's 160 acres, 80 acres and thirty lots of which he donated for public use.

Peter Whetstone had come to Texas in 1830 and fought in the army of the Republic of Texas. He was described by Rip Ford as a man of "great originality . . . witty, the life of a camp though almost uneducated." Through his friendship with Isaac Van Zandt (who named the town of Marshall and its streets), Whetstone further was encouraged to give additional acres for Marshall University. He did so, and the school operated from 1842 until 1884, when Marshall High School was located on the property.

Whetstone became involved in the Regulator-Moderator war (as did most East Texas men); and in 1843, a Colonel Boulware, hearing that Whetstone had threatened his life, shot him down with buckshot—some say at Whetstone's home, some say on the Marshall courthouse square. Whetstone expired instantly. He was not altogether favored by his fellow citizens. One account of his death referred to him as "a noted freebooter . . . and an object of terror and hatred." His grave, not marked, has been lost.

COLONEL WILLIAMS

Although we honor hundreds of early-day Texans, most of our honor goes to heroes of war and of violence. Col. Leonard Goyen Williams, born in 1800, tried to keep peace, not make war, although he had to get involved in that, too. He and his brother, William Williams, came to Texas sometime before the 1820s with their Cherokee wives, planning to live with the rest of the Cherokee tribe near Nacogdoches. Captured by Comanche Indians, the brothers were held captive as slaves for two years. Leonard mastered the Comanche language and in 1822 talked their way to freedom. Leonard returned to Nacogdoches and was given a sizable land grant by the Mexican government for his work in the Fredonian Rebellion. Later, at the Texas colonists' 1835 siege and battle of San Antonio, Leonard Williams lost an eye.

Through his Cherokee wife, Nancy Isaacs, Leonard was considered almost a brother by the Cherokee tribe, and he was sent by Sam Houston to form a peace treaty with the Cherokees under Chief Bowl (or Bowles)—a treaty which prevented the Cherokees from entering the Texas Revolution on the Mexican side. As Williams spoke several Indian dialects, he was able, as Houston's Indian commissioner, to make a number of peace treaties, none of which, it is said, ever was broken by the Indians. (One sees many references to his work in contemporary accounts, but usually he is referred to by the general term "Agent Williams.") Although he ransomed a number of white captives from the various tribes—including two children taken in the disastrous Council House fight in San Antonio in 1841—he never was able to persuade Cynthia Ann Parker to abandon her Indian life, even though he saw her on the prairies more than once.

So intimately connected with the Cherokees did he become that on one occasion he pursued a squad of renegades for miles to apprehend and hang several white outlaws who had been robbing and murdering the friendly tribe.

Colonel Williams was Texas' Indian agent at Torrey's Trading Post below Waco and signed the important peace treaty with the Indians at Tehuacana Creek. When he retired, he spent the rest of his life in or near the town of Mount Calm in Hill County, until his death in 1856. His death was said to have been caused by an old scalp wound inflicted by an Indian warrior. When Williams was on his deathbed, Sam Houston journeyed to his home near Mount Calm to write his biography, but Colonel Williams was too ill to do even this much.

He is buried in Limestone County, "in a cow pasture on land that was his homestead." Neglected for years, the grave of Leonard Williams (and several dozen others) was restored in 1965 with a fund set up to preserve the last resting place of this Texas hero.

THE FIRST BLACK MILLIONAIRE

Without question, one of the most remarkable Texans of the nineteenth century was William Goyens, officially a "free man of color" and possibly the first millionaire in Texas—assuredly the first black millionaire. Born in North Carolina in 1794, of a black father (William Goings) and a white mother, he came to Texas in 1820, reaching Nacogdoches by way of Galveston, "probably with the pirate Lafitte," according to historian R. B. Blake. He remained in Nacogdoches County for the rest of his life, though owning property in other places as well. In 1832, he married Mary Pate Sibley, a white woman; and Benjamin Lundy, the antislavery crusader, who was in Texas at the time, wrote that her brothers visited the Goyenses and approved of the marriage. The couple never had children, although Mary Sibley had a son from a previous marriage.

A remarkably able and shrewd businessman and trader (some of his real estate deals could match modern ones for complexity), William Goyens's wealth originally was based on his work as a blacksmith and wagonmaker, although later, according to Harold Schoen, the "actual labor was relegated to slaves and hired white men, while he [Goyens] engaged in land deals, amateur detective work, raising horses, and litigation." Constantly in danger of losing his life, freedom, and property to fraudulent, conniving white men, William Goyens managed to accumulate an estate ("Goyens Hill") that by 1841 embraced 4,160 acres of farmland (worth $20,600), several town lots, and nine slaves—their ownership thought to be a protective measure on his part. He engaged in thirty lawsuits between 1826 and 1836 alone, acting as plaintiff in fifteen and as lawyer in one. He sued whites success-fully, and in his suits several prominent Texas lawyers enjoyed employment.

He served in the Texas army during the revolution and was an Indian agent and interpreter during a series of 1836–37 treaty meetings with Cherokee and Comanche Indians. He was a good writer and spoke Spanish and Cherokee, as well as several Indian dialects, in addition to English. President Sam Houston recognized the value of his work, but not until 1840 was a free Negro protected (via the "Ashworth Law") from expulsion from Texas—and protected only by petition. Even then, land ownership by a free Negro was not protected. At one point, when William Goyens was in Louisiana, he was kidnapped by a renegade white and forced to give over a Negro woman he owned (or sheltered), as well as to sign a huge note. Upon returning to Texas, William Goyens succeeded in hav-ing it all repudiated. He died in 1856, still free and wealthy, shortly after the death of his wife. They are buried in a Nacogdoches County cemetery.

CHAMBERS' TERRAQUEOUS RAILROAD

There have been hundreds of grandiose schemes proposed in or for Texas, but in scope none surpasses "The Chambers Terraqueous Transportation Railroad Company" of Thomas Jefferson Chambers. This was to be a unique form of trans-portation using some sort of invention not described. As the name indicates, it was for operation on both land and water, and, the charter further pointed out, such use would involve the same "machine." A state charter was granted to Cham-bers (a noted, but not wholly loved, early Texas figure) by the Texas Legislature in 1854 and amended in 1856 with this paragraph: "General Chambers represented he had invented a vehicle capable of traveling equally by land and water, and pass-ing from one to the other with passengers and freight, with speed and safety, equal, if not superior, to first class steamers by water and railroads by land."

The charter gave Chambers the privilege of constructing four thousand miles of road, "to be proportioned out as near as possible, between the different por-tions of the State, and a right of way 300 feet wide to proceed over the land, rivers, and bays of the State." The duration of the charter was one hundred years, but, sad to say, no work ever was done on the "Terraqueous Transportation Railroad."

Chambers County is named for Thomas J. Chambers. He was an important figure in Mexican and Texas land dealings and was made a major general during the Texas Revolution. (He tried to be made a Confederate general, too, but was denied.) An outspoken, flamboyant, and not always straightforward man, he made many enemies in his maneuvering over land titles. As a result of his surveying jobs, at one time he owned nearly 140,000 acres, scattered over several Texas counties. Recognizing the number of his enemies, he built his home, Chambersia, near Anahuac, with an outside stairway to the second floor so that an enemy easily could be spotted. Despite his precautions, he was assassinated in 1865, as he sat in an upstairs room of his home. (The assassin was generally known but was not arrested.)

Years after the general's death, his heirs (two daughters) sued the State of Texas, claiming that the land upon which the state capitol was built actually had been owned by Chambers. The heirs eventually received twenty thousand dollars from the state in 1925.

MARTIN VARNER

Martin Varner, born March 7, 1787, left his Virginia home at an early age after the death of his mother and lived with his two sisters in Missouri. Later he joined two friends and his brother in going down the Mississippi to become trappers in Arkansas. Varner moved to the Jonesborough settlement in Texas, which he helped to found. There, in 1818, he married Betsy Inglish.

When he heard of Moses Austin's colonization plan for Texas, he immediately applied for a grant and in 1821 joined the first group of Austin's colonists, settling at Hickory Point in what is now Brazoria County. Varner's grant was the twelfth issued of the "Old Three Hundred." Varner had the first distillery in Texas. In 1829, Stephen F. Austin thanked him for a bottle of home-made rum, which he called "the first ardent spirits of any kind made in the colony." Varner grew restless in 1834 and sold his plantation to Columbus Patton; (much) later it was bought by Gov. Jim Hogg, whose daughter Ima gave it to the state. Now it is the Varner-Hogg Plantation Museum and State Park.

After fighting in the Texas Revolution, Varner took land in Wood County. In 1843, a neighbor, Simón Gonzales, borrowed money from Varner, putting up some of his tools as security. Gonzales later rode back to Varner's home and asked for return of the tools without repaying the loan. Varner refused, an argument ensued, and the neighbor pulled a gun and shot Varner, reportedly in the back. Seeing his father shot, Varner's only son, Stephen, aged eighteen, ran to the man, who was still on horseback, and grabbed his arm, only to be shot through the heart. A Negro farmer named Joe, a friend of the Varners, appeared on the scene, disarmed the killer, and turned him over to the wounded Varner, who, enraged, cut the tendons in the neighbor's legs, then proceeded to strip him of skin. Varner's wife grabbed a kitchen fork and gouged out the killer's eyes. A neighbor found the man still alive and, as an act of mercy, gave him the coup de grace with a shot to the head. (Descendants say the body was thrown in a hog wallow, from which flooding rains washed it away, and it was never found; others report that it was buried nearby.) Varner died after three days, leaving a wife and six young daughters.

In 1975, a historical monument was erected near the rural homesite, naming Varner as the first Anglo settler of Wood County.

DANCE PISTOLS

Although not the rarest of Texas-made Confederate arms, the Dance revolver occupies a favored position with arms collectors because of its reputation for superior quality and its legendary associations. Even after the centerfire cartridge weapon became standard, many lawmen, Indian fighters, and gunmen refused to give up their Dance percussion pistols. Bill Longley, the Texas outlaw of the 1870s, too young to have been a soldier, was proud of his .44-calibre Dance revolver (serial #4) used in many of the thirty-two killings he reportedly committed.

In 1853, the Dance family had moved to Brazoria County, Texas, from Alabama. In 1858, brothers John Henry, George Perry, and David Etheldred opened J. H. Dance and Company machine shop in the Brazos river-port town of East Columbia. They were not gunsmiths. Their first product was a grist mill, made according to their own patent and adaptable to steam, horse, or water power.

When the Civil War began in 1861, the Dance brothers served briefly as soldiers, then were assigned to work in their own machine shop, at first finishing and mounting cannons, and in 1862 making pistols. Late in 1863, they joined with A. R. Park and his brother Sam to form "Dance & Park." With federal occupation of nearby Matagorda Island, the Dance factory removed to Anderson in December 1863, as that safer town became a military post. (It may be that the move merely combined Confederate activities.) Here Otto and Alex Erichson, sons of famous Houston gunsmith and dealer Gustav Erichson, were assigned to the Dance pistol factory.

For years it was thought that no pistols were made at Anderson, but recent research in records and artifact recovery prove otherwise. The Dance factory also cast cannonballs and converted flintlock muskets to cap-and-ball. The last shipment of twenty-five Dance revolvers to Houston, in April 1865, was broken into, and five were stolen. In May the factory ceased making pistols, and the Dance brothers returned to East Columbia. They never made guns again, turning instead to the manufacture of furniture. When their factory was destroyed in the great 1900 hurricane, it was not rebuilt. David, last of the brothers, died in 1918.

It is believed that no more than 365 Dance pistols were manufactured, including a few rare .36-calibres. Only 80 handguns in all are accounted for, according to Gary Wiggins, whose book, *Dance & Brothers, Texas Gunmakers of the Confederacy,* furnished much of the data for this sketch.

MISSOURI'S CAPITAL

Marshall, Texas, once was the capital of Missouri—at least, capital of its government-in-exile. Upon the death of Gov. Claiborne Fox Jackson of Missouri, on November 28, 1861, Lt. Gov. Thomas C. Reynolds, a Confederate sympathizer, assumed the office. This was not a popular move, by any means, in this border state where, at that point in history, as much blood had been shed over the questions of secession and slavery as anywhere.

Soon after becoming governor, Tom Reynolds met in Marshall with the other Trans-Mississippi (Confederate) governors to chart the courses of their various states. At the end of the conference, Reynolds began his return, via Little Rock, Arkansas, only to learn that the Confederates had retreated from that city. After discussion with his staff, Governor Reynolds decided that Marshall would be a proper alternate site for the capitol. On November 25, 1863, he rented the home of Judge Asa Willie, of the Texas Supreme Court, and from this rather humble domicile Reynolds and staff directed the state affairs of Missouri, as much as they could, through the remaining months of the Civil War. (One must remember that a "loyalist" government remained ensconced in the Missouri capitol at Jefferson City throughout the same period.)

At the end of the war, Reynolds, along with Texas Gov. Pendleton Murrah, fled to Mexico, where Governor Murrah died (in Monterrey) a few weeks later.

The former Missouri capitol was only a frame building, a residence, its importance unrecognized even by local history enthusiasts, and over the years it slowly disintegrated until, in 1950, it was torn down to make way for a medical clinic. A historical marker now indicates where the landmark "Missouri capitol" structure stood.

GEORGE WASHINGTON GRANT

A sad omission of Texas history is the story of Grant's Colony and its benefactor, Col. George Washington Grant. Born in 1814 in Alabama, one of ten children, he possibly came to Texas after 1831, when his father died, leaving him an inheritance of $1,961.22. Records of his land deals near Nacogdoches, dated 1833, can be found. As George Grant was raised in Huntsville, Alabama, and the founders of Huntsville, Texas, named the Texas town for the Alabama town, it may have been this connection that brought him and brother Egbert to Huntsville, Texas, where they operated a stage line.

George Grant was active in land dealing, lumbering, and civic and educational advances. He is credited with starting the campaign that resulted in the creation of Sam Houston Normal School (now Sam Houston State University) in Huntsville in 1879. Earlier he had advocated educational classes inside the state penitentiary. He also was sheriff of Walker County from 1876 to 1878. He developed the town of Grant Springs, setting up a sawmill community there, and at one time he owned nearly ten thousand acres of land in eastern Walker County.

Shortly after the end of the Civil War, George Grant began what he hoped would be a model community of white farmers and newly freed slaves. He named his project Harmony Settlement and located it on his own land some five miles east of Huntsville. Six trustees, apparently (from records) black, led the community. Harmony soon became known as Grant's Colony, and today a road by that name leads to Colony Cemetery, all that remains of the colony itself. He built farm houses, a gin, and a meeting house, and in 1868 the trustees sought land for a school and church house "for the common benefit of all the citizens of Grant's Colony." In 1870, the trustees requested "a site for a school house to be used for the education of freedmen and children irrespective of race and color." Colonel Grant then gave land for Mount Moriah Methodist Church and Good Hope Baptist Church. He leased or rented farmland to the black freedmen, letting them pay rent in cotton or produce. In 1876, during a visit to the Centennial Exposition in Philadelphia, Grant met J. H. Hill, an Indiana farmer, who was demonstrating a knitting machine, and persuaded him and his wife to come to Grant's Colony and manage it for a year. The colony existed for several years but began to break up in the early twentieth century. Little of its history survives. Most family descendants had moved away by the 1930s.

George Washington Grant died in 1889. He and his wife Mary Jane had no children but had adopted a boy and a girl. The vast Grant estate was filed on and mostly dissolved by creditor actions, many of them questionable. Grant supposedly was buried at his residence east of Huntsville, but so strong was opposition to George Grant's Harmony Settlement and his support of freedmen that today the location of his gravesite is uncertain, although a George Grant headstone, with no information, can be found in Huntsville's old Oakwood Cemetery.

KARNACK, TEXAS

Karnack, Texas, is located near Caddo Lake a few miles northeast of Marshall. It was said to have been named Karnack because it was the same distance from Port Caddo (an important port of entry in Republic of Texas days) as Karnak in Egypt was from Thebes. The town has had two distinguished citizens who were father and daughter. The father was Thomas Jefferson Taylor II, born in 1874 in Alabama. He migrated to Texas in the 1890s and married Minnie Lee Patillo, of Alabama, in 1900. Taylor had purchased the fine old (1843) brick home of Cephas Andrews, along with several hundred acres, and it was here that a daughter, Claudia Alta (Lady Bird) was born on December 22, 1912. Her mother died when the daughter was only five years old, leaving two sons and Lady Bird.

T. J. Taylor was famous in the region as a trader and "character," with a brick store in Karnack which carried the sign, "Dealer in Everything." He was considered to be well off. Lady Bird began her education at Fern School, not far from her home. She went to Jefferson High School in Jefferson, Texas, but at age thirteen she transferred to Marshall High School, graduating there in 1928, with the third highest grade average in a class of forty-one members. She then attended Saint

Mary's College in Dallas and received her bachelor of arts and bachelor of journalism degrees from the University of Texas at Austin.

In September 1934, Lyndon Baines Johnson, then secretary to Congressman Richard Kleberg, met Lady Bird in Austin and, as historian Joe Frantz puts it, "in his usual tornadic irresistible style, Johnson 'campaigned' for the young lady's hand." Two months later, on November 17, they were married. They honeymooned in Monterrey and Mexico City, then made their home in Washington, D.C.

T. J. Taylor, in 1934, gave to the state some two-thirds of the land composing Caddo Lake State Park. He died in 1960 and is buried in Marshall.

THE KELLY PLOW

In 1843, John A. Stewart began making plows in a shop operated by a Mr. Sanders in Marshall. In 1848, he moved his plow molds and, with brother-in-law Zack Lockett, began operating a small iron foundry and general repair shop at Four-Mile Branch, a camping ground for ox-team freighters and commercial wagoneers, located west of Jefferson. In 1853, Stewart hired a young Tennessean named George Addison Kelly to be foreman of the iron foundry and plow factory—although the foundry was doing more business in ox- and cowbells than in its crude plows.

In 1854, George Kelly went to Louisville, Kentucky, to learn brazing and more advanced plow making. By 1858 he was a partner with Stewart, adding cast-iron stoves and cooking utensils to their line, and in 1860 Kelly became sole owner, introducing the "Blue Kelly," the first modern plow made in the Southwest. Four-Mile Branch was renamed Kellyville and gradually gained a population of a thousand. During the Civil War, the foundry furnished iron cannonballs (among other supplies) to the Confederate army. After the Civil War, Kelly brought out a successful pony-plow for light-draft breaking of sandy soil. By 1866, he had begun using East Texas iron ore at his furnace, some two miles west of Kellyville. In 1880, a fire swept through the factory. Kellyville had been missed by the railroads, so George Kelly salvaged what he could from the destruction and in 1882 moved the operation to Longview.

In Longview, the Kelly Plow Company soon became the town's largest manufacturing facility—a position it held until the 1930s, when Gregg County (of which Longview is the county seat) became the largest oil-producing area in the world.

As long as Texas' economy remained basically agricultural, "Kelly" was a household word, as well known to farm families as names of nationally famous farm machinery. In Texas, "Blue Kelly" was almost synonymous with "plow." George Kelly died in 1909, but his sons and grandsons operated Kelly Plow Company into the 1960s.

An interesting aside: H. O. Kelly was a highly praised self-taught Texas artist of the 1950s, whose biographer, William Weber Johnson, titled his chronicle *Kelly Blue*. The name was one Johnson applied to a special shade of paint the artist used. Kelly himself never used the name and had no connection with the "Blue Kelly" plow company.

PRESIDENT JEFF DAVIS, OF TEXAS A&M

When Texas Agricultural and Mechanical College was formed, the governor of Texas was made, ex officio, president of the Board of Directors. The honor of convening the first board meeting on June 1, 1875, fell to Gov. Richard Coke, the first Democrat elected Texas governor after Reconstruction. The directors met at Bryan and authorized Governor Coke to offer the presidency of the college to Jefferson Davis, former president of the Confederacy.

C. F. Arrowood, in a 1945 article in the *Southwestern Historical Quarterly*, notes that, on June 14, 1875, Gov. Coke did as authorized. The salary was four thousand dollars per annum, "with [a] residence properly furnished, and as much land attached as might be desired for yards, gardens, etc." Gov. Coke's letter noted, "[I,] on behalf of the State of Texas and all her people[,] ask that you come and live with and be one of us, and make your home and resting place . . . among a people who will never cease to love and honor you."

The appeal by Governor Coke affirmed that "the duties to be performed by the President of the College will not be (defined) until you are heard from." Davis's negative reply was gracious: "No occupation would be more acceptable to me than that which would enable me to co-operate in the organization of a system for the instruction of the youth of our country, in the two important branches to which the colleges at Bryan are to be specially devoted . . . but I should cordially confess that you have overrated my ability and in the consciousness that I could not satisfactorily perform the duties of the office, decline to accept it." Davis did say, if he revisited Texas (he had just completed a visit that spring), he would be glad to confer "on the subject of an education system for Texas; and as a volunteer, to render such service as my small acquirements and shattered constitution may allow."

Ex-President Davis had visited Texas in April, speaking to huge turnouts in Houston on April 12 and in Dallas on April 19. When Jeff Davis visited Dallas, Gen. W. L. (Ol' Tige) Cabell had to get up and ask the crowd to refrain from shaking hands with the former chief executive, as the strength of his right arm, in Cabell's words, "is not equal to the warmth of his great heart." Actually, there had been coolness between Ol' Tige and Jeff Davis during the Civil War. Davis inexplicably refused to promote Cabell, despite heroic reports on Cabell's leadership.

The effort to get the Davis family to move to Texas was a popular one. A movement had been launched in Dallas to raise a fund to purchase a "suitable" homestead for President Davis and to invite him and wife Varina to make Texas their home. Jefferson Davis apparently discouraged such enticements.

Still hoping, in 1878 the Texas A&M Board resolved to ask Davis to attend the first commencement exercises of Texas A&M and deliver "the annual address." Although no record of the invitation or Davis's reply has been found, he did not make the journey. After his 1875 tour, the former Confederate chief never revisited the Lone Star State.

SPINDLETOP TALES

Most Texans know about the famous Spindletop oilfield near Beaumont, where the petroleum age is said to have begun. On January 10, 1901, after many dispiriting years, Capt. Anthony Lucas's 100,000-barrel-a-day gusher came in. (The largest well in the United States previously had flowed only 6,000 barrels.) A famous photograph shows the gusher spouting high above one lone wooden derrick; but within a few months, derricks were so jammed together that, in many cases, their legs intertwined.

But the real story of Spindletop began in 1890, when Pattillo Higgins, a native of Beaumont, began a long crusade to drill "the Hill"—a salt mound three miles southwest of Beaumont, rising ten to fifteen feet above the coastal plain. Several years before, Higgins had put together a financing group for oil exploration, and it was he who contacted Captain Lucas, an Austrian who had experience drilling salt and sulphur wells in Louisiana. In fact, some believe that Lucas himself originally hoped to hit sulphur—which, at the time, had a better market than petroleum. Higgins called his company the Gladys City Oil, Gas, and Manufacturing Company. The "city," which existed only in Higgins's imagination, was named for little Gladys Bingham, a member of the Sunday school class Higgins taught.

In truth, the mound that history knows as Spindletop was not the Spindletop at all. Originally the oil-bearing mound was known simply as "the Hill" or "the Big Hill." Spindletop, before the oil discovery, was the name of a mound two miles east of the oilfield that once had a grove of trees on top of it. One tree in the center of the mound had poked its top above the rest and made the mound and its grove look like the inverted spindle of a top, with the lone tree as the spindle. The tree itself was dead and gone even by the time of the oil strike. The *Beaumont Enterprise* newspaper, in 1901, noting the shifting of the names, remarked, "It happened in the twinkling of an eye [and it] must have been through the means of the fertile brain of a newspaper correspondent or a reporter that the name Spindletop came about."

My great-grandmother, Mary Catherine Dockray Craighead Longley, born in 1862 in San Saba, was a God-fearing woman who, if she sighted another woman smoking a cigarette in public, immediately consigned that sinner to perdition. But from the age of thirteen until her death at age eighty-two, she dipped snuff, as did most of the frontier females she grew up with. When I was a boy, Granny, as three generations called her, used to send me out to find suitably sized peach tree twigs for her to use in making "snuff sticks." Snuff dippers used these sticks, chewed into a brush tip, to massage the snuff into the gums in order to obtain the most flavor from the dip. She also sent me to Roger's Red & White store to get Levi Garrett snuff, warning me to be sure and "feel to see that there are four dots on the bottom." That was supposed to be the strongest snuff Levi Garrett made, although I have always believed this was only a snuff-dipper legend.

Shortly after the Spindletop oilfield began drawing thousands of workers from all over the nation (and the world), Granny and my grandmother Maude Cole (her daughter) followed my grandfather, Ambrose Cole (all three recently had survived the catastrophic Galveston hurricane), to Beaumont, where he went to work at Spindletop, building derricks. Every one of the thousands of wooden derricks of early oilfields had to be constructed by hand.

Somehow my great-grandmother and her daughter managed to open a boardinghouse cafe for the oilfield hands, with their prodigious appetites. Food served was of the simplest sort: potatoes, beans, biscuits, turnips and greens, thoroughly fried beef and pork (chicken, in those days, was a delicacy). No salads, no exotic things like cauliflower, Brussels sprouts, or broccoli. Food was cooked in huge quantities, and some pans were "as big as a wash tub," my grandmother told me.

Lunch (then called dinner) was served in three sittings of thirty minutes each, not for the convenience of my grandmothers, but so that the workers could eat and get back to work without having to wait for dawdlers. Pinto (red) beans, cooked in dishpan-sized enamel vessels, were served at every sitting. Like all the vegetables, the beans were brought to the table in the pans in which they were prepared. Every scrap was gone from the pans after dinner, "just as if some man had picked it up, stuck his face in the pan, and licked it clean," my grandmother remembered.

But one day, at the second sitting, one of the workers asked my grandmother, a pretty young wife, "Honey, can we get some other beans?" My grandmother hurriedly asked my great-grandmother, who ran the house. The answer: there was not an extra bean to be had. The worker, when told, sighed and said okay.

Later, when the hectic dinner had gone through its final sitting and my grandmother was clearing the table, she found the bean pan with a slender island of beans at one end of the pan, atop which, in untouched splendor, lay one of my great-grandmother's snuff sticks which she had dropped from her mouth, unknowingly, onto the beans. Except for the pinto "island," every other bean in the pan had vanished.

JIMPLECUTE **AND OTHERS**

For years people have wondered about the origin of the name *Jimplecute,* given to the weekly newspaper in Jefferson, Texas, which began publication late in 1865. One theory says that, back in the days of hand-set type, an unsober printer, setting the name, set a "pi-line" (all mixed up), or pied the type by dropping the stick—the metal apparatus holding the type. When reassembled, the line read, "Jimplecute." (A problem with this pied-type explanation is: what name was being set in the first place?)

The founder, a man named Ward Taylor, often was asked what the word meant. His answer was, "It describes how I feel at the end of a hard week's work." Another theory says that the name was one given to a mythical beast used to scare slaves, although slavery officially had been abolished in Texas by the time the newspaper began publishing. However, citizens of Jefferson have held *Jimplecute* untouchable. In 1925, new owners from Illinois tried to change the name to *Journal,* but the townspeople wouldn't have it; *Jimplecute* returned.

The Jefferson Chamber of Commerce says that it found evidence a few years ago that a civic drive was started in the days when Jefferson was a major port, and the newspaper was named for the slogan of said drive. Sarah Greene, publisher of the *Gilmer Mirror,* for years the last hand-set daily in the United States, offers the wording of this "official" slogan, and notes that it is on a Texas historical marker adjoining the Jefferson newspaper office. Here is the official explanation: "Join industry, manufacturing, planting, labor, energy, capital, [in] unity together ever- lastingly." If that sounds contrived, blame Ward Taylor's ghost.

Other unusual Texas newspaper names have been the *Bonham Favorite* and the *Jasper News-Boy,* the latter still being published. Dallas' first newspaper was the *Cedar Snag,* which editor J. W. Latimer later changed (one is relieved at the dis- covery) to *Dallas Herald,* no kin to the latter-day *Times Herald.* And nobody can account for the naming of W. R. Lotz's *Callahan County Clarendon* at Belle Plain, in the 1880s.

The first two Texas newspapers (although not printed in Texas) were *Gaceta de Texas* and *El Mejicano,* appearing the same year (1813) with the same editors. The *Telegraph and Texas Register,* founded in 1835 at San Felipe de Austin, was the only paper being published in Texas at the time of the Texas Revolution.

Some of the most colorful newspaper names were found in West Texas in the nineteenth century. Don Biggers' *Billy Goat, Always Buttin' In* of Rotan was "a journal of such things as the editor takes a notion to write." And William Cowper Brann's *The Iconoclast,* in Waco, got the editor killed. Abilene at one time had a newspaper called *The Magnetic Quill,* and Colorado City had *The Josher.*

William Sidney Porter (O. Henry) edited the original *Rolling Stone* in Austin in 1894–95. Edgar Rye, who edited several papers (and wrote some fine mem- oirs) once headed the *Radiator* in Graham. Fort Worth's *Our Bohemia,* the equiva- lent of the "underground" publications of the 1960s and 1970s, appeared in the 1880s.

One of the true success stories of Texas journalism in the 1880s was Alexander Sweet and John Armoy Knox's *Texas Siftings* of Austin, which began in 1869 as a humorous local column, "San Antonio Siftings." Sweet and Knox serialized a feature which became a still-famous book, *Through Texas on a Mexican Mustang. Texas Siftings* became a national institution and in 1884 moved its offices to New York, later opening a London office.

T&P 600 ENGINES

I was born and raised in Abilene, a town which, since its birth in 1881, has been split right through the middle by the Texas & Pacific Railway (now Union Pacific), creating, in effect, two cities: North Side and South Side. I was a south-sider, living only a few blocks from the T&P tracks. From early childhood, I loved the wailing sound of that lonesome whistle and harked to it, feeling the pull as the high-stepping passenger locomotives and the big freight engines roared along, picking up speed and giving off sound as they steamed west past our part of town. Few days were spent downtown that I didn't try to be near the station when the huge black locomotives, whistling and blasting the air with exhaust, came through, pulling a long string of wonderful freight cars with their exotic and romantic names.

I feel as poet Edna St. Vincent Millay did: "Yet there isn't a train I wouldn't take/no matter where it's going."

Although it has been nearly fifty years since the 600 series of steam locomotives ran on the Texas & Pacific Railway, anyone who ever stood beside the tracks and heard (and felt) one of the huge iron horses thunder by can never forget the experience. The 600-series locomotives were the largest steam engines ever regularly scheduled on Texas rails and became the most copied steam locomotives in railroading history. The wheel arrangement—two small wheels in front, five pairs of drivers and two sets of small wheels under the cab—was technically designated "2-10-4." A distinctive feedwater heater, a small tank sitting atop the front of the boiler, was an identifying mark.

Because the 600 series had been designed by and for the T&P, the style became known internationally as the "Texas" engine, even when used on railroads that had no Texas mileage. The 600s were built by Lima Locomotive Works of Lima, Ohio, from 1925 to 1929. Each weighed 735,666 pounds with its tender loaded with 14,000 gallons of water and 5,000 gallons of fuel oil. The locomotive carried a steam pressure of 255 pounds per square inch, and its 63-inch driver wheels were capable of pulling heavy freight trains at sixty miles per hour. The engines were 99 feet long and 10 feet wide. T&P eventually bought seventy of the giants. The first one cost $116,781. Although originally used for heavy freight and oil trains, during World War II, the 600s pulled long strings of troop transports, especially built to accommodate bunks ("side-door Pullmans," Marines and sailors called them), along the 860 miles of T&P trackage in Texas from Marshall to El Paso.

No. 650 was the last of the giants to work on the T&P, and it made its last run on August 12, 1951, pulling a long freight from Marshall to Fort Worth. Scrapping of the 600s began almost immediately thereafter. (The last T&P steamer of any kind was retired in March 1952.) It took eighty thousand man-hours to build (erect) a 600. It could be broken up in forty-eight hours by salvage workers using acetylene-burning torches. The net scrap value was $1,600. For Christmas in 1949, the T&P presented Engine No. 638 to the State Fair of Texas. It had made its last trip in July 1949 between Texarkana and Longview. Unfortunately, the 638 was left unprotected from vandals, and it was virtually wrecked, looted of its engine dials and gauges and other smaller parts. It is ironic that today an operating 600 series locomotive would be worth as much as, or more than, its original purchase price.

Earle V. Brown of Mineola worked for the Lima Locomotive works in Ohio, where the 600s were erected. He worked on the last steam locomotive Lima built in 1952. On the stationary test track, he wrote, "it ran smooth as a sewing machine."

Wayne C. Sellers of Palestine writes: "T&P 600 locomotives were wonders to me. I grew up in Rising Star [Eastland County] where my dad published the *Rising Star Record*. From time to time we would go to Cisco to see the T&P giants roaring through town." (Rising Star had its own railroad for several years, a branch of the Katy, but the town saw nothing so grand as a 600-type engine— only little 4–4–0 "teakettles.")

John Allen Templeton of the Cherokee County Historical Commission says that the last surviving 600 locomotive, No. 610, is stored in the engine house of the Texas State Railroad Historic Park outside Palestine. The 610 Organization, which restored the T&P locomotive, gave it to the Texas State Railroad so it could be protected. As Mr. Templeton points out, locomotives deteriorate quickly when left in the open. The 610 is in beautiful operating condition, shielded from the weather except when pulled out for viewing by rail fans. It is named "Amon Carter, Jr.," for the late Mr. Carter's contributions toward restoring the engine.

The 610 pulled the 1976 "Freedom Train" during parts of its Texas tour and made several fan runs on the Southern Railroad. But it is too heavy to operate on the Texas State Railroad's roadbed. The park does operate a smaller steam engine on daily passenger runs, however.

THE LEGEND OF
IMA HOGG'S NAME

One of the enduring myths of Texas is that James S. Hogg, whom historians consider one of the state's greatest governors, had twin daughters named Ima and Ura or sons Moore and Harry. Jim Hogg indeed had a daughter named Ima, who, as one of the richest, most benevolent women in the nation and living to age ninety-three, probably became better known than her father. But there was never a Ura— or a Moore or a Harry.

The myth of Ura and Ima may have begun in 1890, when Hogg made his first successful campaign for governor. During that whistle-stop tour, eight-year-old Ima supposedly brought along a playmate. The two girls appeared on the speaker's platform, where portly Jim Hogg, who often used his name jokingly, introduced them as his twin daughters, Ima and Ura. However, "Miss Ima," as the world called her most of her life, denied that this ever happened. Miss Ima had three brothers—Will, Mike, and Tom—and no sister. Governor Hogg, after leaving office, was one of the founders of what became the Texas Company (now Texaco), and at his death in 1906, left his children well off.

Why would a devoted father (he was almost too protective of her) bestow such a name on a daughter? Miss Ima said the name came from the heroine of an epic poem by her uncle Tom, a Denton poet and newspaper editor. Texans also have wondered why she never married and thus changed her name. Photos prove her a beautiful young woman, and she was quite a talented pianist.

It has been supposed that Miss Ima, out of family loyalty, was proud of her name; but Virginia Bernhard, Ima Hogg's biographer, discloses that the opposite was true. All her life, says Bernhard, Miss Ima tried to disguise her name, even in her signature, with a nearly indecipherable first name, or tried not to use her name at all: her stationery was printed "Miss Hogg" or "I. Hogg." Often she had her secretaries use their names to make reservations and order items. Toward the end of her life (she died in 1975), she reportedly told a friend, "You know, if I had been born in Scotland, my name would probably have been Imogene." She began calling herself "Imogene." Her final passport was issued to "Ima Imogene Hogg," and a youthful portrait presented to a friend in 1975 is inscribed "From Imogene with love." Did "Miss Ima" represent years of tragedy, despite international fame?

This writer had one visit with Miss Ima Hogg. She was quite fond of architect Wayne Bell, who had worked closely with her in assembling the inventory of old houses at Winedale Historical Center near Round Top. Wayne and I became friends when I took a course in restoration architecture that he taught at the University of Texas at Austin. The class spent a night at Winedale on a field trip.

One day about two months after my first book, *A Personal Country*, came out, Wayne called me in Dallas and said that my wife and I must hurry down to Winedale the next Sunday, as the UT Music Department was giving a concert in Winedale's Four-Square Barn (now the Theater Barn) in Miss Hogg's honor. She had told Wayne she liked my book so much she wanted to meet me. Wayne added, confidently, that she probably would order a thousand copies to give away—that was the way she did things.

We made the trip, not so much for the possible sale of a thousand copies of my book as for the chance to meet the legendary Miss Ima Hogg. The music was pleasant, especially when a lute player explained how difficult it was to keep the instrument in tune, even for one piece of music. At the intermission, Wayne hurried back to my seat and took me up to the front, where Miss Hogg sat. After he introduced us, I squatted down in the aisle by her chair and she put her hand on my head and talked about my book. She asked me if I knew that she once had owned land at Buffalo Gap (the book is about West Texas), and she told me how much her father liked "you people out there." She said to me that she and a little friend had accompanied her father when he was campaigning by rail through West Texas. She said, "That's where people got the mistaken idea that I had a twin sister." The Ima/Ura part of the tale was not mentioned.

I told her how much I admired her and her many gifts to the people of Texas, such as Bayou Bend in Houston and the Winedale center where we were. Since I had grown up with two older women, I also told her, quite sincerely, how pretty she was.

About that time the intermission was over, and half a dozen university officials were trying to have a word with Miss Ima. Gently lifting her hand from my crown (I think she had forgotten it was there), I stood, told her how honored I was, and she once more said she liked my book. I never saw her again—and, so far as I know, the copy of my book that she had read was the only copy she ever possessed.

The
State
of South
Texas

SOUTH TEXAS

South Texas can be another world, a nation within a state, with the vast King Ranch, the mysterious emptiness of certain remote counties, the ancient histories of the river cities that hug the Rio Grande. And, just across that river, Mexican sites that have been vital to the development of Texas.

The ethnic makeup of South Texas is different from that of the rest of the state, with Spanish-surname families living here who go back to the seventeenth century and, along the lower Rio Grande, communities which operate as one on both sides of the river-border with Mexico. "The Border" has its own music, its own myths, and has even developed its own language—so-called Border, or "Tex-Mex," Spanish. Huge figures have risen from South Texas, sometimes heroic, sometimes tyrannical. The myths and legends are strong, and they are not all out of antiquity, either.

South Texans, Anglo and Hispanic, have a reputation for being the most easy-going Texans, living in T-shirts and shorts out on the barrier islands, or crossing in and out of Mexico for trade and entertainment. And in the winter there comes that influx of "snowbirds," travelers from the more northern states and Canada escaping the cold, many returning year after year, often to the same locale or even the same RV park.

The geographical term, South Texas, is deceptive. South Texas ordinarily would reach from San Antonio southward, but border cities such as Del Rio and Eagle Pass along the Rio Grande, while not exactly south, are included in South Texas, and, with the towns around Rio Grande City, make up "the Border." Is Houston south enough to be considered South Texas? Not by some Texans. But neither is Houston nor Galveston truly East Texas, so they are assigned to South Texas. San Antonio is the capital of our "South Texas" state—we must not forget that the national craving for Mexican food, particularly the foods known, like Border Spanish, as "Tex-Mex," began at San Antonio. San Antonio, in addition to its Hispanic heritage, has a vital history of important German and Jewish families reaching back a century and a half.

South Texas stretches along the Gulf of Mexico with Padre Island, from Corpus Christi to Brownsville, a world of its own, self-contained, little dependent upon the rest of Texas. Crossing from "Corpus" (as Texans usually shorten that city's name) to Laredo, you pass through the hot, dry, and lonely range country that has guided the destinies of South Texas since the first Spanish settlements—some villages in South Texas, unfound in hidden corners—go back to the seventeenth century, by tradition—if not by record.

The Republic of Texas was born out of South Texas, with the Alamo, "The Cradle of Texas Liberty," in San Antonio. The Massacre at Goliad took place near that South Texas colonial community, and the defiant "Come and Take It" banner flew at the South Texas town of Gonzales, where the Texas Revolution started. The United States' Mexican War began with the American invasion into South Texas, and because so many American troops landed at Corpus Christi, most of the famous Civil War generals, on both sides, knew Texas mainly from knowing South Texas.

The last land battle of the Civil War was fought in South Texas; during that war, most of the contraband cotton was transshipped from South Texas, via Brownsville and Point Isabel, to Mexico and on to Europe.

There are still large areas of South Texas where time has merely paused and the nineteenth century has not fully expired. There are quiet villages such as San Ignacio, where the official public timepiece is a sundial. There are legendary ranch areas such as Randado or the ghostly "drowned" Mexican city of Guerrero, which occasionally rises to haunt Falcon Reservoir when the water level drops. There are river cities like Rio Grande City and Roma, where their Mexican counterparts, just across the Rio Grande, form a community as important on one side as the other.

Standing half in and half out of both East Texas and South Texas is an informal area which I term the Gulf Coast or Upper Gulf Coast. When Texans refer to "the Coast," it is usually the area that runs south from Houston to Corpus Christi. Below Corpus Christi, of course, the Gulf Coast continues, but reference to it generally is more specific: Padre Island or South Padre, or Port Isabel.

The Gulf Coast includes only towns and cities which are directly on water. These include Galveston and Galveston Island, Freeport, and Matagorda Island, Bay, and Peninsula. The Gulf Coast designation also includes Port Lavaca, Aransas Pass, and Rockport. There are lonesome areas of the Gulf Coast, bays and inlets that still hold secrets, and even today sudden history is emerging. The celebrated site of Sieur de La Salle's lost ship *La Belle,* which came to light only in the 1990s (after three centuries of searching), is on the Gulf Coast, whereas other antique ship discoveries have been along Padre Island.

"The Valley," or the lower Rio Grande Valley, is a third nation within the state, including the multiplex of towns and communities stretching from Brownsville to Rio Grande City, with the complementary Mexican cities of Matamoros, Reynosa, and Camargo. This was one of the oldest areas in Texas, yet it was one of the last to be developed in the early twentieth century.

ICE FOR TEXAS

Almost from the time of its formation as a state, ice-ships, loaded with northern lake ice, visited the coastal cities of Texas. Philanthropist William Marsh Rice, of Houston, made part of his fortune with his brig *William M. Rice,* which imported ice from Boston each summer. One of the complaints the people of Galveston made during the Civil War was that summer ice shipments were cut off by the federal blockade. Blockade runners, carrying guns and munitions, had no room for a delicate cargo that had to be obtained, in the first place, from enemy locations. This led to the first attempts to manufacture ice in Texas.

When the railroads began reaching across Texas in the early 1870s, one of their main cargoes was ice. Packed in cars insulated by sawdust, the ice had been sawed from northern lakes and ponds the preceding winter. The rail cars were able to service cities far from the Texas coast. Although almost forgotten today, the ice crop was as important as was grain in some northern states. In cities such as Dallas, Houston, and Galveston, the finer restaurants advertised that they used "Northern Lake Ice," and in the summers, coal companies in inland areas began selling ice at a competitive price of fifteen cents a pound—which was still three or four times the price of beef or pork.

The melt factor of lake ice was great, so supplies seldom lasted beyond mid-July. Some of the wealthier Texas families built their own ice houses and shipped in private supplies of lake ice.

It was only natural that artificial icemaking and mechanical refrigeration should be pioneered in sultry Texas. In 1862, the second artificial ice plant in the U.S. began operating in San Antonio, coming there via Matamoros, Mexico. A French ice-making machine (developed by Ferdinand Carré) was smuggled through the Union blockade and installed in San Antonio by André Muhl, a native Parisian who claimed that he was the original inventor of machinery to manufacture artificial ice ("by devious means . . . defrauded of the results of his genius and labor," a son declared). Muhl built another machine in San Antonio in 1867 and took it to Waco in 1871 to open the first ice plant there, a business carried on by his sons. In July 1872, an Austin newspaper announced, "Two new ice factories, with a combined capacity of 3,500 pounds per 24 hours, [are] operating on the Colorado River banks," using river water.

In 1865, Daniel L. Holden bought a Carré machine in San Antonio, improved on it, and made an unsung discovery: by using distilled water, he produced clear ice. He and his brother Elbridge, together with Elbridge's father-in-law, George W. Fulton, developed the first refrigerated abattoir in the U.S. at Fulton, Texas, for the purpose of chilling beef for England; the first shipload arrived there in 1880. Refrigerated meat packing and shipping (by boat) was developed on the Texas coast by 1867.

In Dallas, a Lowe carbon-dioxide machine, used to inflate Union balloons during the Civil War (Thaddeus Sobieski Coulincourt Lowe was chief of aeronautics for the U.S. Army), is said to have been adapted to refrigerating beef in 1866, but with no rail facilities at hand—Dallas didn't get its first railroad until 1872—it was a financial failure. Lowe's design was successfully adapted to a ship; however, in fierce competition, a ship equipped by Henry P. Howard, of San Antonio, got the first load of frozen beef to New Orleans in 1868, because Lowe's ship drew too much water to dock. Thomas L. Rankin of Dallas and Denison perfected the first refrigerated rail car, which made the nation's first refrigerated beef shipments by rail in 1873, by way of Denison.

Jefferson, Texas, is considered the U.S. birthplace of ammonia compression refrigeration. There David Boyle, in 1873, established his first plant and, after a fire destroyed his first machine, made arrangements for the Crane Company of Chicago to manufacture an improved model. In 1876, the first of these Crane machines were returned to Texas: to Austin and to Richard King for use in Brownsville and on the King Ranch.

The mechanical refrigeration industry spread in the 1870s. In March 1872, the *Dallas Herald* reported that Capt. Alex McCulloch was in town to form a joint stock company to manufacture ice; the machine to be used was "a Texas invention, the patent being granted to André Muhl, on the 12th of December, 1871." As an inducement to stockholders, "they [are] allowed, for every $100 of stock, to take 10 lbs. of ice per day at the low rate of 24 cents per pound." The first successful commercial ice plant in Dallas began operation in 1878 at Browder Springs, the source of the city's water supply.

Other early Texas ice industry figures included Charles and Andrew Zilker, of

San Antonio and Austin. In 1882, King asked the Zilker brothers to operate the Brownsville plant. Charles Zilker returned to Austin in 1884 and improved on icemaking machinery design, eventually installing ice plants across the South. Austin's Zilker Park is named in his honor.

STEAMBOATS A-COMIN'

Although a number of Texas rivers had boat traffic, most of it was only a paddle-wheel turn or two inland from the Gulf Coast. The Red River, some seasons, carried enough water to take commercial craft to near Paris; and Jefferson, for thirty years, was a heavily used inland port on Caddo Lake. Boats made it up the Sabine as high as Carthage, and sometimes on the Brazos to "the falls" below Waco. One or two times, steamboats actually made it up the Trinity to Dallas and up the Colorado to Austin, and one Brazos boat made it all the way to Cameron (via Little River) from Washington-on-the-Brazos. But in all cases, Texas rivers were dangerous and unreliable. River boat traffic was attempted on nearly every waterway capable of floating even a raft. Remember, there were no railroads in Texas before 1853, and for twenty years after that, mileage was tiny. The development of railroads after the Civil War pretty generally wiped out steamboat dreams.

The one Texas exception to this was the Rio Grande. In the earlier part of the nineteenth century, it had a sufficient water flow and served dozens of small Mexican (and later Texas) towns with small-craft transport. In 1824, a Mexican decree opened the Rio Grande to navigation, and in 1828, a steamboat expedition seems to have reached the falls of the Rio Grande (somewhat beyond Laredo). From that point we have an exciting mixture of legend and fact. First, fact: there was a busy time of several decades on the lower Rio Grande, with steamboat commerce regularly visiting as high up the river as Laredo (an 1890 bird's-eye view of Laredo shows barges being towed). And during the Civil War, Capt. Richard King made his fortune with steamboats, working both sides of the river—and for both sides of the conflict. The last steamboat, the *Bessie,* was on the Rio Grande until 1902. (At least 109 named craft worked the Rio Grande. Richard King alone had 26 boats.)

Nobody knows just how far up the river men got with boats. Some say El Paso, which is questionable unless the craft involved was little more than a canoe. But, as author Pat Kelley points out in his book *River of Lost Dreams,* it was a different

Rio Grande then, usually a full-of-water river, untamed and untortured by the various dams that now cause it to flow, in places, little more than sediment and herbicides.

THE TEXAS HORSE MARINES

Even before the Republic of Texas was formed, the first Texas Navy, while never very large, began a successful career. Like other navies, it quickly found that it needed "soldiers-at-sea," so a Texas Marine Corps was authorized in 1836. Little formal information is available on the corps of the first navy (there were, historically, two different Texas Navies).

The mission of the Texas Marines was to be the security guard of the ship and to make up the boarding and landing parties, and the Texas Marines performed these functions very effectively. Maj. Gen. Marc Moore, of the U.S. Marine Corps (and a Texan), reports that the Texas Marine Corps had certain distinctions: it is the only Marine unit known for which a tomahawk was standard issue, it is the only Marine unit to have been led ashore into battle by the Secretary of the Navy himself, and it may have been the first Marine Corps to be dubbed "Horse Marines"—even though the group that brought about the name was armed rangers and not officially part of the corps.

In June 1836, Maj. Isaac Burton, with twenty or so mounted riflemen, was patrolling the shores of Copano Bay when he saw a suspicious ship sail in. Hiding his men and horses, Burton walked to the beach and signaled the schooner. When a five-man delegation (thinking Burton was a Mexican officer) rowed ashore, Burton's men captured the group; then sixteen of Burton's men rowed out through the surf and captured the ship. Though an American vessel, it was loaded with supplies for the Mexican army—which was still in Texas despite the rout at San Jacinto. When two more schooners were sighted, they were decoyed into the bay—again, American vessels loaded with supplies for the Mexican army. Major Burton and his "Horse Marines" captured them, too, all without a fight. (The ships later were returned to their American owners, but the supplies were kept.) Burton and his men, with horses aboard, triumphantly sailed into Velasco—and, though they were merely rangers, they quickly became known as the Horse Marines.

NAMING VALLEY TOWNS

At the turn of the twentieth century, there were few residents in the part of Texas called "The Valley" (and later "The Magic Valley") northwest of Brownsville. So remote was South Texas that mail between Corpus Christi and Brownsville was carried by stagecoach until July 4, 1904, when the St. Louis, Brownsville & Mexico Railroad (now Union Pacific) began service. Railroads and irrigation put the magic in "The Valley."

By 1903, developing and promoting new towns already had begun along a projected extension of the SLB&M called "The Sam Fordyce Branch," after Col. Sam Fordyce, a railroad backer. J. L. Allhands, in *Gringo Builders,* tells of development along this line. Construction began in 1904. Harlingen ("Rattlesnake Junction") was named by rail builder Uriah Lott for an ancestral city in Holland. McAllen, named for pioneer Anglo rancher, Capt. John McAllen, began in 1903 near an old village called Havana. The rival town of East McAllen sprang up two miles from the original site of (West) McAllen, taking over the name by 1908. La Feria, "The Village Beautiful," was named for its site in one of the oldest Spanish land grants along the border. Mercedes originally was to be Lonsboro, for legendary Valley developer Lon C. Hill; then it was named Capisallo, for the original ranch on which the town was located; finally it was called Mercedes Díaz, honoring the wife of Mexican President Porfirio Díaz, becoming by 1909 just Mercedes. Promoters proclaimed, "No intoxicating liquors can be sold on this land for fifteen years."

Weslaco, begun in 1904, got its eponymous name from the W. E. Stewart Land Company, and Donna was named for Mrs. Donna Fletcher, daughter of landowner T. J. Hooks. Pharr honors H. N. Pharr, of Morgan City, Louisiana. San Juan was named for the San Juan Ranch of John (Juan) Closner, a principal owner of railroad stock. Edinburg originally was Chapin, Alamo was originally Ebenezer. Mission, originally Mamie (for a Closner daughter), was named for Mission La Lomita, of the Oblate fathers, from whom the land was bought. San Benito (1904) was first named Bessie for rail executive B. F. Yoakum's daughter, then the name was changed to Benito (Bennie) to honor Benjamin Hicks, another railroader.

GREAT LINNVILLE RAID

As history subsequently proved, the administration of hot-headed Republic of Texas President Mirabeau B. Lamar (1838–41), while furthering public education, was disastrous in its Indian policy, which was, essentially, "Kill or drive from our Republic." Reversing Sam Houston's conciliatory Indian management, Lamar's aggressive attitude led to the 1839 land-grab expulsion of the Cherokees from their legally assigned East Texas homes and the death of their leader, Houston's friend Chief Bowl.

Nowhere did Lamar's policy prove more costly than in outrageous actions which began in March 1840, at what has come to be called the Council House Fight in San Antonio. There, twelve Comanche chiefs and sixty-five of their followers were lured into a trap by Republic officials for "peace talks," which immediately descended into slaughter and butchery, with the Texans massacring all twelve of the chiefs and killing or making prisoners of all but one of the others as they tried to flee. Seven Texans were killed and eight wounded, including several civilians who fell from indiscriminate firing by their own soldiers.

Seeking revenge, on August 4, 1840, a war party of some six hundred Comanches and Kiowas moved from the hills above San Antonio and began a drive to the coast, sweeping down on totally unsuspecting Victoria on August 6, capturing fifteen hundred horses and mules and killing five men. Then, unlike most Indian raiders, instead of retreating with their loot, they reattacked next day.

The war party, at this point having killed some ten settlers (including the deliberate spearing of a baby), reached Linnville, an important shipping point on Lavaca Bay, with many warehouses filled with merchandise. The town's citizens, unused to carrying arms and located far from the perceived area of Indian raids, thought the Comanches were Mexican horse traders. Thus they were unprepared for the attack which encircled the town, driving most of the inhabitants into the Gulf's waters and aboard boats anchored in the bay. As the surviving inhabitants watched (several had been killed), the Indians spent the day looting and burning the town, destroying or taking everything (including livestock) of value. Linnville never rose from its ashes, and twenty-three Texans were killed during the raid.

The Comanches, celebrating their success over the Texans, became careless and were badly defeated a week later at the Battle of Plum Creek, near Lockhart. In October, an expedition under Col. John H. Moore killed more than 125 Comanche men, women, and children on the upper Colorado River, but scores of Texans paid in blood later. The Comanches and Kiowas became the Texas frontier's most feared and hated raiders, causing depredations which might well have been avoided or greatly lessened, had not Lamar's uncompromising policy replaced Houston's more understanding one, the product of his years of living with other Indians.

SUGAR LAND

William Stafford came to Texas in 1822 as one of Stephen F. Austin's "Old Three Hundred." Like several others, he brought sugar cane cuttings, and in 1834 he built the first Texas sugar mill, a horse-operated affair, at Stafford's Point. But in 1836, while Stafford was gone from Texas (dodging a murder charge which later was dropped), Santa Anna's army destroyed his plantation and sugar mill, which was never rebuilt.

Nathaniel and Samuel May Williams' Oakland Plantation, some five miles away, escaped Santa Anna's wrath, and by 1843 the Williams brothers were producing sugar for sale. This enterprise probably is the oldest one continuously operated in Texas. In 1853, that mill was sold to Benjamin F. Terry (for whom Terry County and Terry's Texas Rangers, of Civil War fame, were named) and W. J. Kyle. They changed the name Oakland to Sugar Land, and in 1856 they constructed the Houston Tap & Brazoria Railroad line to haul sugar to Houston from "The Sugar Bowl," as Fort Bend, Wharton, Matagorda, and Brazoria counties were called. Slave labor was critical in sugar production, and the Civil War ended that first sugar boom.

Terry was killed and Kyle died during the Civil War. Col. E. H. Cunningham bought the Sugar Land mill at auction. By 1890, he had reconstructed the plant, making it the finest sugar refinery in the southern states, and started a town around it, leasing state convicts (then allowed) for cane raising and railroad construction. Cane growing declined in Texas, and in 1902 importation of raw sugar from Cuba and the West Indies began. The Sugar Land refinery was bought in a distress sale by the I. H. Kempner family of Galveston in 1907, and Dan Kempner became president.

While in college, Dan had stayed in New York's elegant Imperial Hotel. Wishing to emphasize quality, Kempner renamed the Sugar Land firm the Imperial Sugar Company. Recollecting the hotel's crest on its stationery, he used a crown as the company logo. By 1925, the huge "char house" (to decolorize raw sugar) had been erected, a Sugar Land landmark for decades. In 1926 the growing of sugar cane ceased in Texas, and in 1928 the last raw sugar mill in Texas (the one at Sugar Land) was dismantled, though the char house remained.

Through the years other major changes took place, not the least of which was the spread of Houston to embrace Sugar Land, which had been a company-owned community. The plant at Sugar Land remained on the same spot where the Williams brothers' mill had operated in 1843. The town incorporated in 1959, after the Kempner family began selling off property, but the old cane fields became Houston suburbs.

In 1973, in the lower Rio Grande Valley, the first Texas sugar cane harvest in nearly fifty years took place, and a new sugar mill there became the Imperial refinery's largest single source of raw sugar. In 1989, the Imperial Sugar Company bought the Holly Sugar Corporation, a beet-sugar processor, and formed the Imperial Holly Corporation.

SWINGING THE FIRST
RAILROAD IN TEXAS

A set of initials familiar to surveyors, petroleum landmen, and geologists is "BBB&C" frequently found printed on survey maps and in legal land titles. The letters stand for Buffalo Bayou, Brazos & Colorado—the name of the first railroad built in Texas. As early as July 1840, grading had been done and ties bought for the Harrisburg Railroad and Trading Company, planned as a transcontinental line starting from Harrisburg (now a suburb of Houston) on Buffalo Bayou. Gen. Sidney Sherman (originator of the cry, "Remember the Alamo!") took over the stalled project, using Boston capital, and in 1848 obtained a charter for the Buffalo Bayou, Brazos and Colorado Railroad. Harrisburg was the eastern terminus and Richmond, thirty miles to the west, was to be the crossing point on the Brazos. The road deliberately was planned to miss Houston, a competitor to Harrisburg.

Work began late in 1852, and the first locomotive, the "General Sherman," arrived at Galveston in December, the second locomotive west of the Mississippi. By August 1853, some twenty miles of rail had been laid to Stafford's Point (now Stafford), which satisfied the BBB&C charter. Service began on September 9.

A *Galveston News* advertisement stated that each Wednesday and Saturday at 9 A.M. cars with passengers and freight would leave Harrisburg for Stafford's Point, returning at noon. There were no Sunday trains. Passengers were carried in four-wheel carriages which originally were Boston horse-drawn streetcars. Riding the rails was such a new adventure that many of the early Texas passengers wrote about their experiences in journals and letters. These show that, despite the perils and torments of ridership (coaches were not weatherproof), the thrill of going twenty miles an hour overcame fear and inconvenience.

The BBB&C finally reached the Brazos opposite Richmond in 1855, and in 1860 it filled out its corporate title by reaching Alleyton on the east bank of the Colorado River, where it stopped until after the Civil War. Most of the mileage of Texas' first railroad remains in operation as part the Southern Pacific system.

Although passenger-carrying railroads were new to the United States (the first one ran in South Carolina in 1831), even a frontier region such as Texas could immediately grasp the enormous benefits from railroads, as contrasted to undependable rivers, and roads that were seldom better than cowpaths. One of the initial acts of the First Congress of the Republic of Texas in 1836 was to charter the Texas Railroad, Navigation and Banking Company. The act was repealed, however, because of its banking provisions. Rail schemes, incited mainly by land grants, continued to be chartered in Texas, but it was 1853 before that first railroad chugged off.

In response to the above "sketch" about the state's first railroad, Tom Jarvis of Dallas sent a copy of a letter penned by his great-great-grandmother, Mrs. Mary Smith, living in Smith County, in 1853. The letter suggests the excitement generated in Texas at the thought of railroads coming. She wrote:

> Last year was an excellent crop year for cotton, lots of it lying at the gins not hauled off to market yet, but this will not be the case when we get Rail Roads, and the time is not far distant till we will have them. Louisiana and Texas is making Wide strides towards it. Louisiana is making one from Vicksburg to Shrevesport [*sic*] thence to the Texas line then Texas has a charter intersecting with that and leading to Elpasso [*sic*] on the Riogrande. [The railroad] is surveyed to Marshall [but] the engineer died and they have sent for another. The charter specifys it to touch Tyler. Louisiana is building another from New Orleans to Logansport, Texas makes it from [there] to Henderson, and another from Galveston to Henderson, thence [to] intersect with the Vicksburg Road between Sabens [the Sabine River] and Tyler.

Mrs. Smith's son, Judge Bennett Smith, lived in Hillsboro, where he died in 1904 at age ninety-eight. The Hillsboro paper once noted, "Judge Smith . . . first voted for Andrew Jackson and is still voting the Democratic ticket."

McKINNEY AND WILLIAMS COMPANY

The Texas Revolution of 1836 was bankrolled by the mercantile firm of McKinney and Williams, formed by Samuel May Williams, secretary of Stephen F. Austin's colony for eleven years, and Thomas Freeman McKinney, who from 1823 had engaged in Mexican trade via Santa Fe, Saltillo, and Chihuahua before joining Austin's colony. The partnership, formed in 1834, helped transport troops and supplies (Sam Houston's army reached San Jacinto via its steamer *Yellow Stone*) and purchased and equipped the schooners *Invincible* and *Liberty* for the Texas Navy. McKinney and Williams (later McKinney, Williams & Company) also issued notes which circulated as the only real money during the provisional government period, and the firm advanced the Republic of Texas some $100,000, little of which was repaid.

The partners formed their firm at Brazoria early in 1834 but soon transferred to Quintana, at the mouth of the Brazos River. The business was moved to Galveston in 1837. McKinney and Williams in 1835 obtained a charter from the Coahuila-Texas (Mexican) legislature for their Banco de Comercia y Agricultura, but not until 1841 did the Republic of Texas validate the charter. Only in 1847 did the bank open at Galveston, the first (and only) chartered bank in Texas prior to the Civil War. In 1837, McKinney and Williams, with Michel Menard, Moseley Baker, and John K. Allen (one of Houston's founders), organized the Galveston City Company. In 1841, the firm launched the *Lafitte,* the first steamboat built in Texas.

Because it purchased so much land script, the name "McKinney, Williams" is found on dozens of surveys in counties as far away from Galveston as Dallas. Bad debts, mostly from cotton brokerage, forced the sale of the mercantile business to kinsmen in 1842 (when the name became McKinney, Williams & Company), but the original partners retained banking. In 1853, McKinney moved to Austin, in effect breaking up the firm, although the name was used until 1858, when

Williams died. Opposition by anti-bank groups had persisted throughout the life of the Commercial and Agricultural Bank, and an adverse ruling by the Texas Supreme Court annulled the bank's charter in 1859 and it was closed.

McKinney died in 1873, a poor man, thanks to Civil War cotton speculation. McKinney Falls, on Onion Creek near Austin, was part of his homestead and since 1976 has been the center of McKinney Falls State Park.

GOLIAD DECLARATION

Although the official Texas Declaration of Independence was signed at Washington-on-the-Brazos on March 2, 1836, and today that date is celebrated as the birthday of Texas, this was not the first such declaration. On November 25, 1835, leaders in Nacogdoches had declared for independence from Mexico; on December 15, at Brazoria, a public meeting endorsed that decision. On December 20, at Goliad, a stronger formal declaration was written and signed.

Goliad, full of Mexican army supplies left earlier by Gen. Perfecto Cós on his way to San Antonio, had been taken by Texans November 9. This loss of supplies contributed more to the defeat of Cós than did Texan arms at the siege of Bexar earlier, in December 1835.

The Goliad garrison, under Capt. Philip Dimmitt, was infuriated by the relatively easy surrender terms imposed on Cós when he surrendered at Bexar (San Antonio). A spokesman wrote:

The undersigned . . . have seen the enthusiasm and the heroic toils of an army bartered for a capitulation . . . no sooner framed than evaded or insultingly violated. . . . They have seen the energies, the prowess, and the achievements of a band worthy to have stood by Washington . . . frittered, dissipated, and evaporated away for the want of that energy, union, and decision in council, which . . . can only be exercised efficiently when concentrated in a single arm. . . . They have witnessed these evils with bitter regrets, with swollen hearts, and indignant bosoms. . . . [Therefore] instead of declaring for "the principles" of Independence, [let us] boldly, and with one voice, proclaim the Independence of Texas. Be it Resolved, That the former province and department of Texas is, and of right ought to be, a free, sovereign and independent State.

The Goliad Declaration, drafted by Dimmitt and Ira Ingramm, his adjutant, was signed by ninety-one men, many later victims, with Col. James W. Fannin, of the March 1836 Goliad massacre. The furious antipathy of the Goliad Declaration was typical of the entire revolution. Self-appointed leaders almost uniformly were uncooperative. With personal antagonism rampant among elected Texas Provisional Government figures, jealousy and envy were such that only a strong leader like Sam Houston could have brought Texas to a successful conclusion of its war with Mexico. And even in the triumph of San Jacinto, Houston had so many enemies among the leadership that President David Burnet proposed deposing him as commander-in-chief when the battle was scarce over.

The Goliad Declaration was sent to the Provisional Government council at San Felipe, but at the time that group retained hopes of securing the cooperation of certain Mexican revolutionists, so the Goliad Declaration was officially suppressed.

DR. JACK SHACKELFORD

Dr. Jack Shackelford (often erroneously called "John") was a forty-five-year-old Alabama physician when he raised a company of fifty-five Alabama volunteers for service in the Texas Revolution. He supplied arms and uniforms, including red jeans, causing the unit to be named "Red Rovers." Dr. Jack and his company landed at Copano Bay in January 1836 and joined James W. Fannin's "Fort Defiance" at Goliad.

In March, after it was known that the Alamo had fallen and Goliad was not to be defended, Dr. Jack, like other leaders among Colonel Fannin's volunteers, urged the commander to speed his retreat. But Colonel Fannin, for reasons history hasn't discerned, dawdled so that even the Mexican Gen. José Urrea was baffled and held off attacking the Fannin forces, thinking they were preparing for a costly stand. But next day, when Colonel Fannin halted his troops on a broad open prairie near Coleto Creek instead of using nearby woods for cover, General Urrea attacked. After nearly two days of bloody fighting, Colonel Fannin, on March 20, signed a surrender document affecting more than four hundred men, including the Red Rovers—at the time the largest Texian army.

General Urrea may have tried to gain clemency for the captured troops, as he claimed, but General Santa Anna ordered all shot, including the wounded. Just before the Palm Sunday (March 27) death march began (three groups were sent in three directions, then each group was executed), Mexican Gen. Francisco Garay came to the mission fortress and took three captive doctors, including Dr. Shackelford, to his tent, where they were kept. Helplessly, they heard the shots and their comrades' dying screams. Dr. Jack's son Fortunatus and two nephews were among the fifty-two Red Rovers killed.

In April, Dr. Shackelford was ordered to Bexar to treat Mexican wounded from the Alamo battle; after the Mexican surrender following San Jacinto, he returned to Goliad. He was so incensed at the "humane" treatment of Santa Anna by Gen. Sam Houston that he went back to Alabama. Although he visited Texas twice more, he never became a resident. His account of Goliad (he kept a diary) is the most valuable original record of the massacre in English. Herman Ehrenberg, an escapee, later wrote a valuable account in German. Shackelford County, in West Texas, is named in Dr. Jack's honor.

R. C. CRANE'S MARRIAGE LICENSE

Royston C. Crane was the son of William C. Crane, longtime president of Baylor University when that school was located in Independence, Texas. Royston was a Baylor graduate (1884) and got a law degree from the University of Texas in 1886. He became a noted lawyer, judge, newspaperman, civic leader, and historian in the West Texas towns of Roby and Sweetwater.

In 1884, as the June class of Baylor graduated, a Sweetwater physician was on campus to claim Genoa Cole, a Baylor teacher, as bride. In the wedding party was Mamie Douthit of Sweetwater, a teenager whose beauty and charm attracted Royston Crane. He kept up with her, but it was several years before he felt capable of asking for her hand. Finally, in 1892, he won his suit. He was living in Sweetwater, but by then Miss Douthit's family had moved from Sweetwater to McKinney to Quanah to Velasco, and he had to go to that Texas Gulf Coast port to gain his bride.

There was then no railroad to Velasco, so he went by rail to Columbia, then took a boat down the Brazos River past Brazoria, the county seat where he planned to get a marriage license. He made the first two legs of his trip, but the boat failed to stop at Brazoria long enough for him to see about the license, so he asked a college friend, who was disembarking, to see W. S. Bittel, the county attorney, and have him obtain the license and send it to Velasco by the evening mail gig along the river trail. Attorney Bittel had graduated from Baylor with Royston Crane, so Crane felt sure he could depend on him. But that night, when he called for the mail, the license had not arrived. He was told that it might have gone on to Quintana, the end of the mail line. In desperation, Crane went to the livery stable, hoping to hire someone to go to Quintana. There he found a schoolmate from Independence in charge. This friend offered to go by horseback to see about the license. At Quintana, the postmaster turned out to be a man who had boarded at the same place as Crane during his law school days at Austin. The Quintana postmaster opened the post office, and there was the license. The document was immediately dispatched by horseback to Velasco, arriving there at 1 A.M. The wedding took place at 7 A.M., in time for the bridal pair to catch the boat back to Columbia and thence the train home to Sweetwater, after an enormous series of school-inspired chance encounters.

Their son, Royston C. Crane, Jr., who was born in Abilene in 1901, created the syndicated comic strips "Wash and Easy" and "Captain Easy," and then, in 1943, "The Adventures of Buz Sawyer," about a Navy airman and his crewman, Roscoe Sweeney. The latter strip was carried in almost one thousand newspapers worldwide.

THE ALAMO'S LAST MESSENGER

Although he is known as "the last messenger from the Alamo," John William Smith played more important roles in Texas history—and was not the last messenger from that doomed garrison. (At least twenty messengers were sent from the Alamo by Col. William B. Travis. Herman Ehrenberg, a Goliad survivor, wrote that Travis repeatedly sent messages to Col. James L. Fannin, asking for help.)

A Virginian who had come to Texas in 1830, John William Smith settled in Bexar (San Antonio), where he became a merchant and the only civil engineer in the region—as well as a Texian spy. In October 1835, when the Mexican Gen. Perfecto Cós marched his troops into San Antonio, he conscripted Smith to work as an engineer. Unbeknownst to Cós, Smith kept detailed notes on the locations and strength of the Mexican fortifications. The notes were given to Ben Milam and Francis W. Johnson, commanders of the Texas troops in the December 1835, siege of San Antonio, and are credited with enabling the Texas forces to outmaneuver and outfight the larger Mexican forces, bringing about the surrender of Cós after five days.

Remaining in San Antonio with the Texian garrison, John William Smith, despite being forty-four years old, served Colonel Travis as scout and messenger, and he and Dr. John Sutherland brought the first word of Santa Anna's large army marching on San Antonio. The siege of the Alamo began on February 23, and it was Smith who managed to slip the thirty-two Gonzales volunteers into the Alamo on March 1. It is said that Smith, as final messenger, left the Alamo at midnight of March 3 and crawled on hands and knees beyond the Mexican lines, carrying not only official communications to the Provisional Government at Washington-on-the-Brazos, but also many private letters from Travis and others to friends and relatives. Smith arrived at Washington-on-the-Brazos on March 6, the day the Alamo fell. Historian Walter Lord says there is "overwhelming evidence" that another messenger, sixteen-year-old James L. Allen, was actually the last to leave the Alamo. He rode bareback from the Alamo after nightfall on March 5 with a final appeal for help to Colonel Fannin at Goliad. Young Allen survived Goliad and became an honored judge and mayor of Indianola.

Smith fought in the battle of San Jacinto and, upon returning to San Antonio, became the first elected mayor in January 1837—a position he held two more times. He was serving in the Texas Congress as a senator when he died of influenza in January 1845.

THE ALAMO MONUMENT MESSAGE

Since the battle of the Alamo in 1836, the most famous epitaph for that historic occurrence has been "Thermopylae had her messenger of defeat; the Alamo had none." Who originally said it?

The phrase first appeared carved on the original Alamo monument, which was the work of English artist William B. Nangle and Joseph Cox, a stonecutter. William Nangle had come to Texas before the Revolution and in 1839 was eking out a living in San Antonio, carving small mementos from stones taken from the Alamo.

Captain Reuben Potter suggested that Nangle make a suitable commemorative from Alamo stones. With the aid of stonecutter Cox, sometime after 1841 Nangle finished a ten-foot-tall monument.

Soon afterward, Nangle died, and the monument was put on display by Joseph Cox at Galveston, Houston, and New Orleans, where exhibition fees were insufficient to cover costs, and the monument was lost for eight or nine years in a New Orleans marble yard. A man named Cavanaugh bought it "for a song" (according to Reuben Potter), and it was displayed in the vestibule of the new capitol in Austin in 1855. In 1858, the Texas Legislature voted to purchase it for $2,500.

But who first uttered the phrase that graces the monument? In 1894, Dr. R. C. Burleson said that it had been delivered by Gen. Edward Burleson, speaking at Gonzales shortly after the Alamo siege. In 1898, a writer to the *Texas Historical Association Quarterly* (now *Southwestern Historical Quarterly*) credited Gen. Thomas J. Green with the quotation. Nonna Smithwick Donaldson, daughter and amanuensis of Texas memoirist Noah Smithwick, in a later issue of the *Association Quarterly,* pointed out that General Green didn't arrive in Texas until a month after he supposedly made the speech. She suggested that it was Gen. Thomas J. Chambers. In 1904, yet another voice, Alex Dienst, gave three other possible sources for the line. Since then, no one has offered more light.

As for the monument itself, it was burned in the capitol fire of 1881, but the ruins were acquired by the Daughters of the Republic of Texas and have been displayed in the Old Land Office Building in Austin. The "new" Alamo monument on the capitol grounds was dedicated in 1891 and bears the names of those defenders who died in the battle. Forty of the names are reported to be inaccurate.

INDIANOLA

Although most parts of Texas have what might be called ghost towns—communities left behind by mining or the oil business, or farm villages that died when the railroad or the highway missed them—there are other, more prominent ghost towns that once played distinct roles in Texas or even national history.

Historically, the most important was Indianola, in Calhoun County, a harbor also known as Indian Point, Karlshaven, and Powderhorn. Of Indianola, the first edition of the *Handbook of Texas* says, "Of the many ghost towns of Texas, none lived longer, none throve better, none died as tragic a death."

A natural port on Matagorda Bay at Indian Point was called Karlshaven, in honor of Prince Karl of Solms-Braunfels, when German immigrant groups were entering Texas in the early 1840s. Shortly after that, the port became the major entry and depot for the United States Army, because it was the closest port to San Antonio, military headquarters for Texas. The famous U.S. Army camel experiment in 1856, using camels instead of horses and mules for southwestern desert transport, landed its animals here.

Historian John Henry Brown claimed that the name Indianola came from his wife, Mary, when Brown became editor of the first local newspaper there in 1852.

Indianola was a pioneer site in the Texas canning industry, using beef, turtle, and turkey as its products. By 1859, Indianola had its own railroad to Victoria; and after the Civil War, despite having been taken and looted twice by Union forces, had grown to a population of six thousand, which, for the time, was of major city size for Texas. The first frozen beef shipment in American history left Indianola for New Orleans in July 1869. The Indianola Railroad, which was built as one of the few broad-gauge railroads in Texas (rails 5 feet, 6 inches apart) was converted to standard-gauge (4 feet, 8-1/2 inches) in 1870. It became the Gulf, Western Texas and Pacific, connecting with the San Antonio & Mexican Gulf, but it was abandoned in 1887, after the hurricane of 1886 destroyed both the town and the railroad headquarters and facilities.

Indianola, in its time, was the second most important port in Texas, behind Galveston. But in 1875, the low-lying city was hit by a typhoon which destroyed most of the town. It rebuilt, but only partially, and by 1886 rail competition out of Galveston was crippling its port trade. That year the second, even more disastrous hurricane finished Indianola. It was abandoned. Today the site of Indianola is marked mainly by a state park and some huge brick cisterns planted in the earth.

S. RHOADS FISHER

The rough-and-tumble first years of Republic of Texas government are well illustrated in the career of Samuel Rhoads Fisher, signer of the Texas Declaration of Independence and first holder of the cabinet post of Secretary of the Navy. He was appointed by President Sam Houston in 1837, even though Fisher had been a supporter of Stephen F. Austin in the first Republic of Texas election. (Today it seems impossible that there should have been competition between Houston and

Austin, the two most important figures in Texas history—but such is human nature and ego.)

S. Rhoads Fisher, born the last day of 1794, was a rather wealthy Philadelphia Quaker who brought his family to Texas early in 1832, settling at the then-important port of Matagorda. He planned to trade salt and tobacco to Mexico for hides, using schooners he controlled. In 1833, Fisher was made *alcalde,* or judge, erecting a small courtroom near his home to accommodate this responsibility.

In 1835, when Texas' revolt from Mexico broke out, Fisher led twenty Marines in taking over a prize vessel from the Mexican navy but was accused of private speculation by young James W. Fannin, Jr. Fisher, overreacting, attempted unsuccessfully, with a vituperative broadside, to provoke Fannin to a duel. (Duels plagued early Texas government.) Fisher was a delegate at the convention which wrote the Texas Declaration of Independence, but his twelve-year-old daughter Annie's scarlet fever caused him to miss the March 2 signing by several days.

Fisher, while Secretary of the Navy, against Houston's orders sailed with the two remaining ships of the Texas Navy, the *Brutus* and the *Invincible,* raiding Isla de Mujeres, a Mexican island off the coast of Yucatán, and burning eight or nine small Mexican towns and capturing several ships, including a British ship. Both the *Brutus* and the *Invincible* were lost crossing the bar while attempting to re-enter Galveston Bay. President Houston, hearing the news of Fisher's foray, promptly declared that the Republic of Texas was not making war on Mexican peasants or performing "other acts not calculated to elevate us in the scale of nations." He fired Fisher from his cabinet.

A battle ensued between Houston and the Texas Senate over whether or not a president could dismiss his appointees without senate approval. Eventually, as was usual when Houston was involved, the case became politically bitter. Fisher was accused of embezzling $1,100 from the Republic, which was not proven. Fisher finally was allowed to resign, still believing that he had staved off a Mexican invasion with his "the best defense is a good offense" tactics.

Fisher, notoriously short-tempered, was shot and killed in Matagorda by Albert G. Newton in 1839. Newton was no-billed. Fisher County is named for Samuel Rhoads Fisher. No satisfactory biography exists of this most unsung of all the important figures of early Texas history.

THE GREAT WESTERN

One of the most colorful and least known figures of Texas and United States history was Sarah Bowman, or Borginnis, or a couple of other names. (She was married, or changed partners, several times.) She stood six-one or six-two and, from the time of the Mexican War, was recognized throughout the U.S. Army as "The Great Western." The nickname seems to have come from the name of the first successful trans-Atlantic steamer, which was the world's largest when launched in 1837.

George Washington Trahern, who knew her in the Mexican War, reported, "She was a great nurse, and always went with Taylor's army in Florida and Mexico; she stood six-foot-two and kept a sort of restaurant . . . headquarters for everybody. She was an immense woman, would whip most anybody in a rough and tumble fight." When a scared soldier told her (inaccurately) that the Mexicans had defeated Taylor's army and were on the way, reportedly she "drew off and hit him between the eyes and knocked him sprawling," cursing him and saying, "You just spread that report, and I'll beat you to death."

Technically a laundress, she was admired for "virtuousness," although at least once she ran a hotel and brothel. Several times she took up arms, at other times loading cartridges, dressing wounds, and carrying off wounded soldiers in the midst of fierce fighting. Rip Ford recorded, "She had the reputation of being something of the roughest fighter on the Rio Grande and was approached in a polite if not humble manner."

Following the Mexican War, she had been deserted, while sick, in El Paso del Norte (now Ciudad Juárez) by a U.S. unit on its way to California and "had since passed through much privation, suffering and hardship," she said. In 1849, when Lt. W. H. C. Whiting and his engineers were crossing the Rio Grande to go to El Paso del Norte, they saw The Great Western as she was heading for the U.S. side in a canoe. He wrote, "Never was anyone more delighted at the sight of American officers . . . her masculine arms lifted us one after another off our feet." Later that year she moved across to Texas and opened a hotel at Ponce's Ranch, where gold-seeking "Forty-Niners" testified to her kindness.

She died of a poisonous insect bite at Fort Yuma, Arizona, in 1866, at age fifty-three, and was buried with full military honors in the U.S. Army's Fort Yuma cemetery—the only woman ever so honored. In 1890, the bodies in that cemetery were exhumed and reburied in the national cemetery at the Presidio in San Francisco. Her tombstone carries the name "Sarah A. Bowman."

JOHN HENRY BROWN

One of the early, but still generally reliable, Texas historians was John Henry Brown, son of Henry S. Brown, a pioneer Texas soldier for whom Brown County is named. Son John Henry, a Missouri native (born in 1820), learned printing there before coming to Texas in 1834 after his father's death, to live with an uncle, James Kerr, one of Austin's "Old Three Hundred."

John Henry Brown was a frontier ranger for some years, then moved to Austin in 1840 to work on the *Texas Sentinel* but left to serve as a minuteman under Col. Jack Hays. In 1843, visiting Missouri, he married another visitor, Mary Mitchel of Groton, Connecticut, returning with her to Texas to work on the *Victoria Advocate*. In 1848, he established the *Indianola Bulletin* and began his career as a historian with the "Early Life in the Southwest" series for *DeBow's Review*. In 1854, he co-edited the *Galveston Civilian,* was twice mayor of Galveston, and represented Galveston County in the Texas Legislature. He was strongly proslavery. He edited the *Belton Democrat* in 1860 and represented Bell and Lampasas counties in the 1861 Secession Convention.

During the Civil War, John Henry Brown was on Gen. Ben McCulloch's staff until McCulloch was killed. Then Brown was given command of a Texas frontier district. Brown fled to Mexico at the end of the Civil War and remained there five years, serving for a time as commissioner of immigration for Emperor Maximilian, settling Americans, mainly former Confederates. His book, *Two Years in Mexico, or, The Emigrant's Friend,* printed by the *Galveston News* in 1867, sold ten thousand copies.

In 1871, Brown moved to Dallas and built a "country" home at Live Oak and Pearl—now in the heart of downtown Dallas. After representing Dallas County in the Constitutional Convention of 1875 and serving as city alderman, he was elected mayor in 1885, serving two terms. Undoubtedly he was the most erudite mayor that city ever had, although politically his tenure was stormy. But it was as a historian that Brown earned his lasting fame. In 1881, he edited the *Encyclopedia of the New West* and in 1887 published a *History of Dallas County*. His *History of Texas from 1685 to 1892* and *Indian Wars and Pioneers of Texas* were published in the 1890s. All are rare in original editions.

John Henry Brown died in Dallas in 1895.

"PRINCE JOHN"
MAGRUDER

John Bankhead Magruder was a Virginia native (born in 1807) who graduated from West Point at age twenty. During the Mexican War, he was made lieutenant colonel and afterward was stationed at Newport, Rhode Island, then (as now) one of the social capitals of the nation. Here he entertained so often and so lavishly that he became known as "Prince John," sporting whiskers and a vigorous mustache "in the English manner." Prince John also designed his own uniforms.

In 1861, he was appointed a general in the Confederate army and defeated a small Federal force in the Battle of Big Bethel, possibly the first land battle of the Civil War. However, his lack of control under battle conditions cost the Confederate forces dearly, even in victory, and after the Seven Days, he lost favor with Gen. Robert E. Lee.

In 1862, Magruder was sent to Texas, where he commanded the district which included Texas, New Mexico, and Arizona. In smaller engagements, Magruder showed his superior generalship. On January 1, 1863, he staged a brilliant and successful defense of Galveston and in November stretched a thin line of Texas troops along the Gulf Coast to successfully repel federal occupation of Texas. His troops contributed to stopping the so-called "Red River" invasion attempt by Maj. Gen. N. P. Banks in 1864.

At war's end, although he had surrendered his Texas troops, Magruder, ever one for the grand gesture, refused to live under what he called "foreign rule" and fled to Mexico, joining Maximilian's army as a major general. After Maximilian's execution, Prince John returned to Texas, settling in Houston in 1869, where he died in 1871, being buried in Galveston. Prince John was married to a wealthy wife, but so seldom was he with his wife that most Texans, including any number of young women, thought that he was single.

Prince John has a unique historical honor. During the Mexican War, he was stationed for a time at Corpus Christi, where he built a theater to put on plays and so keep soldiers out of trouble. As a result, U. S. Grant was probably the first U.S. president (there have been others since) to have had experience as an actor. Magruder talked Grant into playing Desdemona in an all-male production of Shakespeare's *Othello*.

GENERAL SHELBY
BURIES THE FLAG

Although called an "expedition," the Shelby Expedition of 1865 was closer to being a retreat—an attempt to escape what Gen. Joseph O. Shelby of Missouri and half a dozen other diehard Confederate leaders thought surely would be their fate: death, imprisonment, or revenge of another sort.

Shelby was in command of the Missouri Iron Brigade, which was stationed in Marshall, Texas, at the time of Appomattox. Shelby had been offered a Union commission at the beginning of the war but had turned it down contemptuously. At the end of the Civil War, Shelby refused to surrender and took his command to Mexico in the "Shelby Expedition."

A powerfully persuasive man, he was able to lead a unit estimated at several hundred men across Texas, via Waco, San Antonio, and Eagle Pass, and into Mexico, hoping to gain the support and enlistment of Maximilian. The "expedition" was studded with Confederate brass: Texas Governor Pendleton Murrah was included, as were Missouri's Gen. Sterling Price and Confederate Gen. "Prince John" Magruder. Two other confederate governors and several lesser politicians (as well as some wealthy private citizens) went along. The troops levied upon the country as they passed, creating a certain amount of hostility, the war being over and supplies none too available.

When the group started to Piedras Negras, across the Rio Grande from Eagle Pass, with great ceremony they reverently folded and weighted their Confederate battle flag with Texas and Missouri stones and "buried" it in the river. This act, or ceremony, has come to be called the "Grave of the Confederacy" incident. At that point, Shelby allowed his officers and men the opportunity to offer their services to either Benito Juárez or the Emperor Maximilian. Knowing that the United States government was opposing the emperor, the diehards voted to support Maximilian.

Marching in military order to Mexico City, they were subjected to numerous guerrilla attacks on the way and eventually disposed of many of their arms to Juárez. When they arrived in Mexico City in August 1865, their offer of aid to the French impostor was refused, Maximilian being afraid that any favoritism shown to ex-enemies of the United States might lead to further problems with that nation. However, certain individuals were given lands to colonize. The so-called Confederate colony in Córdoba was named "Carlotta" after the Empress. Shelby occupied the hacienda of General Santa Anna but later moved to a Confederate colony at Tuxpán, working as a freighter-owner.

Although several of the Americans remained in Mexico, most left within two or three years. Among the latter was Gen. Jo Shelby, who returned to Missouri, where he died in 1897.

LAST SHOT OF THE CIVIL WAR

Although Lee's surrender at Appomattox took place on April 9, 1865, in effect ending the Civil War, it took some time for word to spread—or to be accepted by all the Confederate commanders. In Texas, Confederate troops held Brownsville and, although newspaper reports of Appomattox had begun to circulate early in May, Confederate Gen. James E. Slaughter and Col. Rip Ford were undecided about what to do. When, on May 12, word reached them that 1,600 Union troops under Lt. Col. David Branson were marching toward Brownsville from Brazos Santiago Island, off the coast, Slaughter suggested that it was time to retreat. Ford, pounding the table, however, declared, "Retreat, hell! We're going to fight!"

That evening there was a skirmish at Palmito Ranch, twelve miles east of Brownsville. Believing that Confederate reinforcements were on the way, Union troops burned the ranch and fell back some four miles to Palmito Hill. Next morning Rip Ford arrived with a battery of six 12-pounder cannons and at 4 P.M. began an advance. The union troops—who knew that the war had ended—either retreated or surrendered, most hurrying back to Brazos Santiago. They suffered 111 deaths and a number of casualties.

That was the last battle of the Civil War, but the last shot had not been fired. Brian Robertson, in *Wild Horse Desert,* tells how that happened. That night, while the Confederate forces waited, uncertain as to what to do next, a federal gunboat, the USS *Isabella,* sitting in the Rio Grande, fired a cannon shot which exploded near a seventeen-year-old boy. He picked up his rifle and, cursing at being disturbed, fired one bullet in the direction of the gunboat. That was the very last land shot fired in the Civil War.

Union prisoners finally convinced their Confederate captors that Lee had surrendered, and, on May 30, 1865, Gen. E. B. Brown took over Brownsville in the name of the United States.

EARLY BEEF PACKING

Although cattle raising was always important to Texas, it was not until after the Civil War that intense efforts were begun to find ways to get beef to world markets. The 1867 *Texas Almanac* describes one new method which seems akin to modern freeze-drying (and perhaps foretells the popularity of mesquite broiling).

The Stabler Patent Beef-Packing Co. has been started in Indianola and . . . we have had a conversation with the patentee, Mr. Francis Stabler, of Baltimore, Md., and from him we have learned the particulars of the process. The beef is cut up into steaks, the bone taken out, a small quantity of salt put on and allowed to stand three hours to draw part of the moisture from the meat. It is then put into cans, weighing from fifteen to fifty pounds, which cans are put into an iron box, which can be made airtight by the quick motion of a screw. The air is then exhausted by means of a column of water, and carbonic acid gas introduced in the place of the air, [t]hen the cans are soldered up and are ready for shipment to any part of the world. This process possesses this decided advantage, that by two hours' soaking in water you can have as good a broiled steak of Texas beef, in any part of the world, as though you were on the mesquite range of Texas, and at a lower price to the consumer than the salt beef of the Western States of Ohio, Indiana, and Illinois, which has had the juices soaked out by the brine.

Carbonic acid gas, used in this process, is the same that is in daily use in all families. It is owing to its presence that our bread gets its lightness; our ale foams in its presence; and when indulging in the more extravagant luxury of a glass of champagne, we reap our reward by the sparkle *this gas* gives . . . A board at the Brooklyn Navy Yard examine[d] the meat and reported that they "found the properties of the meat . . . better than any other they had seen; they cooked it in various ways and in all it was juicy, tender, palatable." This will eventually have the effect to make stock-raising one of the most profitable branches of our home industry.

It is interesting to note in this report that, at this early date, Ohio, Indiana, and Illinois not only were considered "western" states but also were competing with Texas beef for the U.S. market.

ESCANDÓN'S COLONIES

One of the greatest Texas colonizers seldom is recognized by latter-day historians. He was Spanish-born José de Escandón, who in 1746 was appointed governor of Seno Mexicano (Mexican womb), that deserted strip involving most of South Texas below the Nueces River.

Although ranching was taking place in scattered spots along the Rio del Norte (Rio Grande), little was known of the area. In 1747, Escandón organized a great seven-part expedition of 765 soldiers to explore the region. The various groups mapped 120,000 square miles and, in the words of historian Brian Robertson, "managed something almost beyond the comprehension of the modern world," without the loss of a single man.

One group, under Capt. Miguel de la Garza Falcón, entered Texas near Eagle Pass and mapped the north bank of the river down to today's lower valley. Nuevo León groups from Cadereyta, Linares, and Carralvo, under Carlos Cantú, moved along the southern bank of the Rio del Norte, while two groups traveled northward along the Mexican coast from Tampico. Joaquín de Orobio Bazterra left the Texas mission La Bahía del Espíritu Santo, near Goliad, and moved southward, while Escandón himself led an impressive group to near the present site of Brownsville. Escandón was especially successful with Indians, incorporating several as friendly allies and guides.

The newly explored region was renamed Nuevo Santander and, in 1748, potential settlers were offered free land, two hundred pesos for supplies, a travel bonus, and no taxes for ten years. Asking for five hundred volunteer families, Escandón got seven hundred. Eventually, many towns along both sides of the Rio Grande were settled, including Mier (at the historic Cantaro crossing, where ranching already was taking place), Camargo, and Reynosa.

In 1750, the first Escandón-inspired settlement north of the river was made at Dolores, ten leagues southeast of present-day Laredo. Then, in 1755, the last townsite, Laredo, was settled under Capt. Tomás Sánchez. By 1755, some 6,384 persons were in twenty-three settlements made through Escandón's impetus. He died in Mexico City, accused of swindling, but later, through the efforts of a son, his name was exonerated.

Mrs. Velia Shiflett of Dallas is a descendent of one of Escandón's senior officers, Blas María de la Garza Falcón, brother of Miguel, and reports that several branches of the family still are well represented in the Rio Grande Valley area. The

Texas town and the modern lake on the Rio Grande are named for the Falcón family.

PORT ARTHUR

Port Arthur, the inland Gulf port that now is an oil refining and chemical center of some sixty thousand inhabitants, was established on a hunch. Despite its location in one of the oldest settled areas of the state, Port Arthur is a "newer" Texas city, coming into existence only in 1895. Arthur C. Stilwell, the Kansas City railroad builder and founder for whom it is named, had projected a line from Kansas City through Arkansas and Louisiana to the Texas Gulf. (He sold railroad stock in Holland, which is why places named Mena, DeQueen, and Queen Wilhelmina Park are found in western Arkansas.)

Learning that an existing railroad to Galveston was for sale, Stilwell went to New York and secured an option to buy it, calling a meeting of his directors to ratify the purchase. But he wrote in his memoirs (quoted in S. G. Reed's *A History of the Texas Railroads*):

> Then I had a hunch—one of the wierdest. I became possessed of an overpowering fear that we were planning wrongly . . . because of the storms of tremendous violence that lashed [the Gulf Coast] at times. An intuitive sense—or a hunch as I have chosen to call it—told me to abandon the entire project and look for a more northeasterly portion of the Texas coast for the end of our line to deep water . . . and there occurred to me a picture of a city of 100,000 persons on Lake Sabine . . . [a] landlocked harbor, safe from the most devastating storm the Gulf could produce.

Next day he advised his directors to pass up the existing rail line and approve his original plan, which they did. Within thirty days he had acquired fifty thousand acres on the north bank of Lake Sabine, laid out a town on four thousand acres, and named it Port Arthur. He later sold the remaining acreage to rice farmers, organized the Port Arthur Ship Canal and Dock Company (selling the stock in only one day), and then built the seven-mile canal connecting the lake with the Gulf to make a deepwater port. After the discovery of oil at nearby Spindletop in 1901, Port Arthur quickly became a world refining center and a leading United States port.

Stilwell was an unusual person. Amid his developmental activities, he also wrote poems, novels, financial guides, and semi-mystical works explaining his personal beliefs and defending his career from what he called "the Wall Street cannibals."

Arthur Stilwell's other great Texas scheme was the Kansas City, Mexico and Orient Railway, from Wichita, Kansas, through West Texas to Presidio and thence across northern Mexico to the Pacific port of Topolobampo. The road was completed after many setbacks, and Stilwell was forced out; but it paid off only during the oil boom along its line below Fort Stockton. The KCM&O (usually called "the Orient") was taken over by the Santa Fe in 1928, and in the 1970s and 1980s was abandoned, in most stretches, so that by 1990 only a few miles were still in use.

Stilwell, or his companies, established several other Texas towns, including Nederland, near Beaumont; and Rochester, Hamlin, and Rule in West Texas.

BAGDAD

Although it lay across the Rio Grande in Mexico, the city of Bagdad [*sic*] played an important role in Texas history during the Civil War, when it was the largest cotton shipping point in North America. Boca del Rio, as it was called by natives, was built in 1780 by colonists from Matamoros, some twenty-five miles inland, who planned it as a summer resort. Legend has it that the name Bagdad came from the pirate Jean Lafitte.

Although the Union navy succeeded in blockading the Texas coast, by treaty with Mexico it could not stop navigation on the Rio Grande. Cotton was floated over from Texas to Mexico and then shipped out from Matamoros and Bagdad to Europe. Texas entrepreneur Mifflin Kenedy kept twenty-six steamboats busy on the river, under the Mexican flag, during the war. Ten stagecoaches ran daily from Matamoros to Bagdad, which had a wartime population estimated at thirty thousand. William Marsh Rice (whose will created Rice Institute) shifted his business operations from Houston to Matamoros during the war.

Of course, Union agents, as well as Confederates, were plentiful in Matamoros and Bagdad, and Texas trader Charles Stillman, working though a Mexican agent, sold goods to both sides. Father P. J. Parisot, an early Bagdad pastor, wrote, "The cosmopolitan city was a veritable Babel, a Babylon, a whirlpool of business, pleasure, and sin."

A small boat could pick up twenty to forty dollars a day hauling cotton out to the merchantmen three or four miles out in the Gulf. Raphael Semmes, the Confederate captain of the raider *Alabama,* wrote of Bagdad, "Numerous shanties had been constructed on the sands. Some were hotels, some billiard-saloons, and others grogshops. The beach was piled high with cotton bales going out and goods coming in. The stores were crowded with wares. The panorama looked like some magic scene which might have been improvised in a night."

In 1867, a hurricane wiped out much of the town. Rebuilt, Bagdad was wiped out again in 1874, this time so thoroughly there was nothing to rebuild. Today most of the townsite is under water, with no sign of the former sinful city.

HOUSTON'S RIVER OAKS

River Oaks, Houston's elite residential section, came into being because one oil-man didn't want to live near another oilman. In the early 1920s, a fashionable development known as Shadyside had sprung up north of Rice Institute (now Rice University), attracting, among others, J. S. Cullinan, the founder of Texaco. Will Hogg, son of former Texas Gov. Jim Hogg, was ready to build a mansion there, but, according to the late famed architect John Staub, Will had had a falling out with Cullinan (a former oil partner) and did not want to live in the same area with him. Hogg, therefore, decided to create his own subdivision.

Will and brother Mike, along with Hugh Potter, Will's former roommate at the University of Texas, bought 1,100 acres of raw land along Buffalo Bayou west of downtown Houston and began developing "Country Club Estates." Their enclave for the affluent was to have wide, winding lanes, parks, and cul-de-sacs, and all sales and house plans were to be approved by the Property Owners' Association. By the time ground was broken in July 1924, Country Club Estates, as well as the main boulevard and the country club, had become River Oaks, and three million dollars were being spent on the amenities.

Mud was so deep that two truckloads of rubber boots were ordered for prospective buyers to wear while looking. Although the smallest lots (64 by 140 feet) could be bought for two thousand dollars, it was a tremendous price in that day. The Hogg family—Will, Mike, and sister Ima—reserved the largest lot of fourteen and a half acres, where Ima, according to her biographer Virginia Bernhard, commissioned Staub to produce the twenty-two-room showplace that, between 1927 and 1928, became Bayou Bend (now a museum). Will and Mike, like Ima unmarried, had their quarters in the east wing, complete with tap room and a gymnasium. In 1929, Mike married Alice Frazer of Dallas and moved next door. Will died unexpectedly in 1930.

River Oaks today remains Houston's most celebrated neighborhood, having numbered among its residents such noted Houstonians as "Silver Dollar Jim" West, Will Clayton, Hugh Roy Cullen, Oveta Culp Hobby, heart transplant pioneer Dr. Denton Cooley, and the late Gov. John Connally.

THE OLD THREE HUNDRED

Although by 1820 Anglo settlers were already in Texas—including some living in Nacogdoches and San Augustine and along the Red River in the northeastern corner—the original families settled by Stephen F. Austin, called the "Old Three Hundred," are accorded a status in Texas history similar to that of *Mayflower* ancestors in New England.

Austin originally was given permission to settle three hundred families in 1821 and quickly began bringing colonists to Mexican Texas. Those three hundred were mostly in place by August 1824, but a few titles were not issued until 1828. The choice grants of the first settlers were the rich bottom lands of the Brazos, Colorado, and St. Bernard rivers.

Early grants extended up the Brazos as far as present-day Brazos County, and they concentrated around colonial headquarters at San Felipe de Austin and at the old Atascosito crossing in modern Austin County. Some eighteen modern counties were involved in Austin's grants. No limits were designated for Austin's original colony. Everything lying between the Gulf of Mexico and the Old San Antonio Road and between the Lavaca and the San Jacinto Rivers was considered within the grant.

Families were given no less than one *labor* (about 177 acres) or one *sitio* (about 4,428 acres), according to whether they were farmers or stock raisers. Unmarried men could join in partnerships of two or three to constitute a "family." Some men, such as James Cummins, John P. Coles, and William Rabb, got larger tracts for erecting grist mills. Jared E. Groce, the richest of the "Old Three Hundred," was given ten *sitios,* on account of the large amount of property he brought with him to Texas, which meant chiefly slaves. Most families coming in 1821 and 1822 received extra lands, also. Austin and the Mexican land commissioner were not limited in the amount of land they could claim.

GENERAL SHERIDAN'S APOLOGY

One of the most famous remarks ever made about Texas came from Union Army Gen. Philip Sheridan, military governor of Texas and Louisiana for a period during the Reconstruction era. He bitterly compared Texas and Hell as places of residence, saying that if he owned them both, he'd rent out Texas and live in Hell.

The remark has achieved such legendary status that some historians, in and out of Texas, have questioned whether it actually was made by Sheridan or if the words were put in his mouth by later writers. But in 1880, on a visit to Galveston accompanying former U.S. President U.S. Grant, "Little Phil," as he was called, admitted to making the quip but attempted to explain it away. Sam Acheson's book, *35,000 Days in Texas,* describes how it happened.

Speaking at a public dinner at the Tremont Hotel, honoring him and President Grant, Sheridan's talk was filled with sentiments flattering enough for any Texan. In conclusion, he told his (mostly) ex-Confederate hosts:

> Speaking so kindly of Texas—and I speak from the heart—probably I ought to explain a remark I once made about it. It was in 1866, and I had just returned to San Antonio from a hard trip to Chihuahua on some Mexican business, when I received an order to proceed at once to New Orleans. I hired relays and coaches so that I had only to hitch on the wagon and go speedily to get the boat from Galveston.
>
> I traveled night and day. It was in August and, need I say, very warm. I arrived here covered with dust, my eyes and ears and throat filled with it. I went to a little hotel in that condition and had just gone up to the register when one of these newspapermen rushed up to me and said, "General, how do you like Texas?"
>
> I was mad, and I said, "If I owned Texas and all Hell, I would rent out Texas and live in Hell." Needless to say, that did not represent my true opinion of this magnificent State."

Sheridan was given a standing ovation.

The
State
of North
Texas

NORTH TEXAS

Geographically, North Texas, like Central Texas, is more often defined by its neighbors than by specific boundaries, except for the Red River. This indefiniteness exists both on the map and in the minds of other Texans—or, maybe, in the minds of North Texas residents themselves. You seldom hear someone proclaim, "I am a North Texan," the way West Texans (sometimes too proudly) want to exclaim to one and all, "I'm from West Texas." And if you do hear a brag about North Texas roots, the voice will most likely come from one of the smaller towns, like Bonham, Honey Grove, Greenville, or Wolfe City. Even Fort Worth likes to say (or used to) that it is "where the West begins."

There are plenty of organizations and institutions carrying the North Texas name, such as the University of North Texas (fourth largest university in Texas) and associations ranging from the North Texas Arabian Horse Club to the North Texas Regional Clearing House Association. Clear regional identity, however, is often lacking. An example is the former East Texas State University, which, despite the school name, is not truly in East Texas. The city of Commerce, where the university is located, is much more North Texas than East. In any case, the school is now Texas A&M University at Commerce, a regionless identity.

Part of the reason for this uncertainty about North Texas is Dallas and its huge economic influence—so huge, in fact, that it enjoys a separate designation, "The Metroplex," a useful term created by a Dallas advertising man. Fort Worth, lying fewer than thirty miles to the west of Dallas, does not consider itself to be part of the Metroplex, if that designation is taken to favor Dallas. (By now, however, the term has become so familiar that it has lost its exclusive Dallas association.) Fort Worth retains a semi-separate, if unpopular, designation in the term "D/FW," sometimes used by non-Texans to refer to the two cities' combined metropolitan areas. To residents of North Texas, however, "D/FW" is solely the name of the big airport lying halfway between the cities of Dallas and Fort Worth—one of the busiest airports in the world, by the way.

In general, North Texas, as a separate "state," stretches across the north and east top of Texas from Texarkana to Wichita Falls and from the Red River down to an indistinct line that weaves itself above and below Interstate Highway 30. There are other large cities in North Texas—Denison, Denton, Mount Pleasant,

Paris, as well as Sherman and Sulphur Springs—but North Texas' population is centered around Dallas and its environs, including the suburban cities of Garland, Richardson, Plano, Irving, Grand Prairie, Terrell, and Waxahachie, some of which were mere interurban stops until the 1960s. Combining Fort Worth and Arlington with Dallas, this North Texas "state" becomes the largest Consolidated Metropolitan Statistical Area in Texas (although few North Texans pay much attention to such governmental configurations).

Properly speaking, Texas should have a separate Northeast Texas, the old entryway of pre–Republic of Texas settlement. Davy Crockett and his Tennessee Boys came to Texas by way of Northeast Texas. Texarkana and Clarksville certainly need the Northeast designation, while, just a few miles south, Atlanta, Daingerfield, Jefferson, and Winnsboro usually are considered parts of East Texas.

Wichita Falls, and Wichita County and its neighboring counties to the east, are flexible. They can accept membership in the State of North Texas but more properly might like to be Northwest Texas, if they are not going to be included in West Texas. As a matter of fact, the so-called boundaries of North Texas are crumbling every year, so that the definitions are shrinking in some directions and expanding in others. Many of the former limits are now mainly historical. In that respect, North Texans have fewer traditional traits, which may reflect the origins of the area's early settlers, who came as much from Illinois, Missouri, and Tennessee as from the Old South. In 1861, the tier of North Texas counties along the Red River voted overwhelmingly not to secede from the Union.

The historic role of North Texas has been as the mercantile and manufacturing center of Texas. Storekeepers learn to be all things to all people, and North Texas finds customers all over the world. Dallas, with its fine symphony orchestra and Dallas Theater Center, traditionally has assumed for itself the role of cultural leader of Texas—though not without a good deal of deserved back-talk from Houston. Fort Worth, once called "Cowtown," saw its streets trodden by cattle on the Chisholm Trail in the nineteenth century and later was home to a number of wealthy West Texas ranchers. But the meat-packing industry and its stockyards gave "Cowtown" its true definition; these defining features departed, by stages, over a period of some twenty years. Today, Fort Worth has become Texas' most quietly sophisticated city, with famous art museums, unique downtown attractions, and the state's first subway—still free for riders.

The Dallas–Forth Worth "Metroplex" is home to more professional athletic teams than any city in Texas. North Texas audiences annually set attendance records for football, and often for basketball or baseball, too. Dallas has become the home of dozens of retired athletes, especially veterans of the popular Dallas Cowboy teams.

THE MILITARY POST
OF FORT WORTH

Construction of a United States Army post on the West Fork of the Trinity River was begun in May 1849, by Maj. Ripley Arnold, with Middleton Tate Johnson, of Johnson's Station (now Arlington) as guide. It was the northernmost in a line of forts which began west of San Antonio and continued northwest of Austin, the Waco Village, and Dallas. One of its duties was to enforce a line beyond which settlers were not to extend and below which Indians were not to intrude.

Major Ripley Arnold's company of forty-two dragoons first camped at the Cold Springs near the Trinity River, but a July flood sent the troops scrambling up a bluff to higher ground. There, after dispossessing civilian Press Farmer and his family, who were living in a tent on the proposed military site, the soldiers began building Camp Worth. It was named for Gen. William Jenkins Worth, commander of U.S. forces in Texas, who had died about the time construction began. Camp Worth was designated Fort Worth in mid-November.

The post consisted of twenty buildings, including stables. All were of logs and, according to an inspector's report, were leaky and insubstantial. Lt. W. H. C. Whiting, an engineer, complained (officially) that the stables were "much too near the quarters . . . and cannot but be offensive in summer." Major Arnold was a dashing aristocrat who brought his wife Catherine and their five children to the post in the summer of 1850, her piano accompanying her. But the summer was a sad one for the Arnolds, as two of their children died. Major Arnold, who spoke excellent French, employed Adolphe Gouhenant (often referred to as "Dr. Gounah"), of New Icaria, the ill-fated utopian experiment in Denton County, to teach his officers swordsmanship and social dancing. As a result of bureaucratic delay, the U.S. Army post of Fort Worth had little to guard, the Indians of that area having moved farther west and northwest. Fort Worth was abandoned in September 1853. At that same time, Maj. Ripley Arnold, on duty at Fort Gates, was shot and killed by a fellow officer, who was not punished.

Fort Worth was located on land which today lies immediately west of the Tarrant

County Courthouse in downtown Fort Worth. When the army moved out, many settlers moved into the fort buildings, and several of the city's most important pioneers began their residency in Fort Worth with the boon of this free rent.

Fort Worth saw only one military engagement—and it was won with a single shot. In 1850 a large group of Taovaya (Wichita) warriors attacked a smaller group of friendly Tonkawa Indians just across the Trinity River, west of where the fort perched atop a bluff. The Tonkawas, who had performed scouting duties for the post, begged the soldiers to protect them from the Taovayas, and a detachment rode out and escorted the Tonkawas to safety. This made the Taovaya chief furious, and he led his six hundred or so warriors up to the outpost, demanding that the refugees be surrendered immediately and threatening to attack the fort if they were not. (Fort Worth did not have a high wall and gate for protection but was merely a group of buildings around a parade ground.)

Major Arnold knew that his tiny garrison would be severely damaged in such a fight, so he used psychology, of a sort. Boldly challenging the Taovaya chief to come right ahead, Major Arnold directed that the post's one small cannon be loaded and fired at a wooden door which was set up as a target some distance from the fort. When the shell whizzed past the Indians and blew the heavy wooden door into a thousand pieces, the warriors needed no further argument. Indeed, the chief said, almost apologetically, that he and his tribe were just wanting something to eat. Three beeves from the military herd were given the tribesmen, and next morning they were gone. That was the peaceful outcome of the only hostilities Fort Worth experienced.

RED RIVER NAVIGATION

A long-lasting dream of the northern Texas pioneers was navigation of the Red River. Many early settlers did, in fact, manage to reach Texas by way of the Red River. Skipper Steely, in his book *Six Months from Tennessee,* tells of the tribulations undergone by the Claiborne Wright family in 1816, as they brought a keel boat from Tennessee to Pecan Point, an area in North Texas then disputed to be Miller County, Arkansas. By 1820, there were dozens of American families living on both sides of the Red River (although Texas was still a Spanish province), and small boats and rafts were regularly used to transport goods, generally downriver but sometimes as far upriver as modern Denison. The early (1815) city of Jonesborough, in modern Red River County, had a boat landing until the river shifted to nearly a mile away.

Travis Wright's Kiamatia Plantation, farther upriver in Red River County, opposite the Kiamichi River's mouth across the Red in the Choctaw Nation, was considered the head of navigation on the Red, although a Paris (Lamar County) furniture factory kept a steamboat at Arthur City, on the river near Paris, for delivering wood, and operated it into the twentieth century.

A U.S. Army Corps of Engineers report of 1900 says that, prior to the Civil War and for some years thereafter, the Red River was the scene of a busy steamboat traffic. (However, this report seems overly enthusiastic.) Between 1848 and 1861, the Red River lines included large steamers such as the *Caddo, H. M. Wright,* and *Grand Duke,* running between New Orleans and Shreveport. From Shreveport smaller packets ran to Jefferson (Texas), at the head of Cypress Bayou, reaching there via Caddo Lake below the great Red River Raft, a miles-long accumulation of logs and other debris which limited river navigation above it to much smaller craft. Suggesting how formidable a barrier the Great Raft was, the insurance rate below it was 1 percent of value, while above Whiteoak Shoals, which marked the raft, the rate was 3-1/2 percent.

Capt. Henry Shreve, whose work camp became the city of Shreveport, used slaves during a pre–Civil War government project to open the river. He was, at best, only partially successful, however, and fever carried off several workmen. A passage was finally cut through the Great Raft in 1872, after nearly forty years of huge costs in finances and lives.

The Red River never was reliable. After the 1870s, railroads rapidly built through the Red River Valley in all directions, and by 1887 boat trips above Shreveport were, the Corps of Engineers report stated, "rare and almost unknown." That 1900 report sighed, "Whether river trade above Shreveport (to Kiamatia landing and Fort Towson) may return to antebellum proportions is a matter of conjecture, but it appears doubtful, to say the least." The report pointed out that the Red "is strewn with the wrecks of steamboats, more than a hundred lying in the channel between Fulton, Arkansas, and the mouth." Fulton, located near where the Red River becomes the border between Texas and Arkansas, had been founded by Stephen F. Austin in 1819. It was the final named "head of navigation" port on the Red River; but in 1899, only one stern-wheel steamer, the 87-ton, 105-foot *Waukesha,* made the stretch to there and made only fifteen round trips with a total of 217 passengers.

McKENZIE COLLEGE

The earliest Texas colleges were church schools, usually begun by a minister. Although some colleges (academies) were more nearly high schools, the courses offered might daunt modern students: Greek, Hebrew, Latin, rhetoric, oratory, philology.

Typical was McKenzie College, opened in 1841 near Clarksville, in northeastern Texas. The president was John Witherspoon Pettigrew McKenzie, a University of Georgia graduate and a Methodist minister who, because of health, had to retire as a missionary in Indian Territory (Oklahoma). His first school building was a log cabin about sixteen by eighteen feet. On one side a log was left out, forming a window. McKenzie College was coeducational, and two dormitories were named "Graft" and "Duke" for the carpenters who built them. Sixteen students, many "little more than children" (according to one of Reverend McKenzie's daughters), enrolled the first year. Enrollment gradually increased, however, so that many older persons—some beyond usual college age—were students.

Four students were lodged in each dorm room. Sometimes they were forced to study in shifts throughout the night, as all four could not crowd around the single oil lamp on the one table and still benefit from the fireplace.

Chapel services were held at 4 A.M. and again in the evening. Classes opened with Bible reading and prayer. Any class in which young ladies were enrolled was presided over by a married man. Students had to pledge, on their honor, not to play cards, billiards, or unlawful games; not to leave the grounds or be out of their rooms during study hours; not to be absent or tardy at prayers or class recitations; and not to keep firearms, smoke, drink whiskey, or attend "any exhibition of immoral tendency, including dancing parties." Despite strict discipline, few boys were expelled, and never a girl.

McKenzie College grew to be one of the most important Methodist schools in Texas and by 1861 had three to four hundred students. Most of the prominent Methodist ministers in North and Northeast Texas attended McKenzie College (or Institute). Tuition was $189 for ten months—and that included room, board, and laundry. The McKenzie family, led by the Rev. McKenzie himself and including daughters and a son-in-law, were part of the faculty or the administration.

By the summer of 1861, most of McKenzie's male students had gone into the Confederate army, and the school began offering military drill as a course. By 1863, the enrollment had dropped alarmingly, and, although McKenzie College continued until 1868, after graduation of that year financial distress closed the school permanently.

DENTON'S
WANDERING GRAVE

In May 1841, John B. Denton, an itinerant Methodist preacher and lawyer for whom the county and city of Denton are named, was killed from ambush by Keechi Indians at the battle of Village Creek near present-day Arlington. His grave was to wander for the next sixty years.

Denton's death came as a consequence of his own rashness. He struck out in advance of the group he was with, remarking that his fellow soldiers seemed to be afraid to pursue the tribesmen across a creek. He fell from a bullet fired by an unseen foe. His body was carried from the battle site by his discouraged fellow Texans, who retreated northward for twenty-five miles, and for the next two decades the body lay in a stone-lined but unmarked grave on Oliver Creek near the town of Justin.

In 1860, Denton County rancher John Chisum, whose father, Claiborne Chisum, had taken part in the Village Creek fight, disinterred what some survivors believed were Denton's remains (mere bones), and Chisum buried the remains in a tin box in a corner of the yard of his ranch headquarters northwest of Denton. Although Chisum did not mark the new Denton grave, he gave directions for finding it. He sold his Denton County ranch in 1866, moving to West Texas and then New Mexico. He died in 1884.

In 1901, the Pioneer Association of Denton County, after what it termed "considerable investigation," declared its official acceptance that the bones in the tin box were Denton's remains. The bones, having been exhumed once again, were reburied in great ceremony in the southeastern corner of the courthouse lawn in Denton, where they rest today, marked with a suitable monument.

There has been much question as to the authenticity of the bones buried in the county courthouse grave of John B. Denton—whether they are, in fact, Denton's bones. It was reported that the grave Chisum opened in 1860 did not match the description of the stone-lined grave or its location as reported in 1841, and that the bones found were Indian bones. Chisum himself questioned whose bones they were, hence his casual treatment of the reburial. Some historians based their questions on testimony offered in later years by Henry Stout, a survivor who was wounded when Denton was killed. Stout and a party revisited the original grave site. The former militia captain told reporters why he did not believe it had been where Denton was originally buried. Considering this strong evidence that Denton's grave was not found by Chisum, the reporters suggest that his bones remain somewhere north of Arlington, possibly near the village of Westlake, but, appropriately enough, in Denton County.

LONESOME DOVE

The Lonesome Dove Baptist Church, located northwest of Dallas, is the oldest church in Tarrant County. It was organized in the cabin of Charles and Lucinda Foster Throop in February 1846, with twelve charter members, including Baptist minister John Freeman and his wife Nancy. The first meetings were held either in homes or outdoors. A church house was erected in 1847. The present Lonesome Dove Church building sits on that original site. Tradition has it that some large rocks under the church are stained with the blood of an Indian who was killed in an unrecorded raid. The rocks were seen in 1869, when the first church was torn down, and the story was repeated in a sermon at an 1891 Old Pioneers Reunion. In 1930, when the church building burned, members told of seeing the blood-stained rocks again.

There are several versions of how Lonesome Dove Church was named. The most romantic says that the members met outdoors under an oak tree, and, as they were praying for guidance, a dove lighted nearby and began cooing, inspiring the name. Another version is that this church, so remote in the wilderness, was God's lonesome dove. There also may have been a church of similar name back in Missouri, where most of the founding members came from.

Z. N. Morrell, in his famous nineteenth-century book, *Flowers and Fruits in the Wilderness,* tells that, in 1849, Lonesome Dove joined with churches at Rowlett's Creek, Union (near Carrollton), and Bethel (Collin County) to form the Elm Fork United Baptist Association. Noah Byars, in whose building at Washington-on-the-Brazos the Texas Declaration of Independence was signed, often preached at Lonesome Dove Church.

In 1985, Texas author Larry McMurtry titled a novel *Lonesome Dove,* after he saw the name on a bus, not knowing its source. McMurtry's novel and the television miniseries based on the book created a great deal of interest in Texas history. Some readers ask how historical and how "Texan" the story is. The book is fiction, thus none of it is literal history; but it is very Texan. McMurtry is a Texas native, as are William Wittliff of Austin, who scripted and produced the miniseries script, and Tommy Lee Jones, who played Ranger Call in the miniseries.

Dallas lawyer Jim Watson suggests that Captain Call is partly based on Ranger Capt. L. H. McNelly, who killed Juan Flores, "who is clearly," Watson says, "the historic figure on whom Pedro Flores, of *Lonesome Dove,* is based." Some incidents on the trail drive in *Lonesome Dove* (shooting the sodbusters and burning the bodies, for instance) are mentioned by Teddy Blue (E. C. Abbott) in his book *We Pointed Them North* and by some old cowhands in *Trail Drivers of Texas.* In this latter book, the name Xavier Wanz (*Lonesome Dove's* saloonkeeper) is found—although Wanz was a prominent rancher, not a saloonkeeper.

The return of Gus's body to Texas is based on the 1867 saga wherein Charles Goodnight and assistants, to fulfill a promise made to the older partner, laboriously returned the body of Oliver Loving for burial in Weatherford, after Loving had been mortally wounded in a New Mexico Indian fight. The infamous Blue Duck name comes from an outlaw associate (or lover) of Dallas's own Belle Starr, after she fled Texas for Indian Territory.

There was a Texas trail driver named Jake Spoon, who was quite different from ex-Ranger Jake Spoon of the story. In the story he was hanged for his association with outlaws. The real Jake Spoon (1864–1922) was reported by the *Menard News* to have made ten trips up the trail and died on a cot in his front yard in Menard, where he is buried.

PANTHER CITY

The rivalry between Dallas and Fort Worth, which went on for more than a century, seems about over now, except for some good-natured nudges now and then. One aspect of the ancient feud lingers on, however: nicknames. Fort Worth is now, and probably will be for the next hundred years or so, known by a name a former Fort Worth resident gave it: "Panther City." (Fort Worth is also known as "Cowtown," but that nickname has become less and less apt, as the stockyards are closed and packing houses have left town.)

"Panther City" came about much earlier than "Cowtown." The Panic of 1873 had stopped the Texas & Pacific Railroad at Eagle Ford, six miles west of Dallas and thirty miles short of Fort Worth. (The railroad didn't reach Fort Worth until 1876.) The lack of a railroad hit the frontier town hard, and by 1875 only about one thousand persons remained in the city.

A Dallas lawyer, Robert E. Cowart, visited Fort Worth, where he formerly practiced, and reported to the editor of the *Dallas Herald* that things were so dead over there in that city to the west, that he actually had seen a panther asleep by the courthouse in the middle of the street. Dallas and the newspaper made much of the story—this was evidence that Dallas was booming while Fort Worth was dying.

But Fort Worth turned the tables on Dallas. Instead of denying the panther tale and sulking, Fort Worth picked up on it proudly. Pretty soon nearly everything in Fort Worth was being called "Panther"—from saloons to meat markets. It wasn't long until Fort Worth was billing itself "Panther City," and when the state's first professional baseball league, the Texas League, began in 1888, the Fort Worth team was the Panthers, and the name stuck, changed slightly to the Cats, until the Texas League came to an end in the 1960s. Today a number of Fort Worth firms use "Panther" in their corporate names.

ANTI-SOUTHERNER

Not every Confederate man was full of enthusiasm for the Civil War and its purposes, as a personal note in the extremely rare set, *A History of Greater Dallas and Vicinity* (1909), shows. David C. Nance, the writer of the note, who edited the biographical sections of the above work, lived in Dallas County and said he had been in Texas since age ten. Much opposed to slavery, he came to hate himself for joining the Confederate army. Nance speaks of the infamous Dallas Fire of July 1860, which slavery advocates claimed was set as the first step in a slave insurrection. They used it as an excuse to terrorize both slaves and white persons opposed to slavery—and to hang three "guilty" slaves. Whatever the cause of the fire, there was no insurrection, nor any evidence that one was planned.

Nance seems to assume that, even before the Civil War, slavery was already headed for extinction:

> In 1860 the question of slavery was on top[,] and designing slaveowners and [slave] traders saw their doom—and by intrigue they sought to deceive and

so postpone the evil day. Accordingly an imaginary insurrection among the slaves was announced far and near by these men and their dupes. Imaginary incendiaries [they claimed] had passed through in the night and had counseled the slaves to rebel—and the poor black men were rounded up like cattle and whipped without mercy. The object of the whipping was two-fold: first, on the part of the traders, to bring down the price of slaves in North Texas; second, to discourage betimes any possible real insurrection.

The writer was present at one of these whippings, though he took no part in it. And even now, after all these years, it makes his blood run cold when he thinks of the horrors of that day. He knew the young men who used the lash [and] the only one who exhibited any mercy is also the only one who has made any success in life. One of these merciless men perished in the first [Civil War] battle he was in; a second perished in the next; the third was later whipped to death in the penitentiary; a fourth, who did not use the lash much . . . is without a home and without even one friend in all the earth.

And if there is any one act of his whole life [this writer] regrets more than another it is entering the army. He regrets it first because he wishes he never assisted in the protection of an institution so fraught with evil as that of human slavery; second, because war is murder and murder has no mercy in it. And here [in the army], like he humbled the men who used the lash, God also humbled me. For it is a fact . . . that the very first ball ever fired at [the] brigade, as also the very last ball, each hit me. There were other events quite as strange, all connected and made to speak and have a meaning to me. They said, "You must show mercy to men."

It was brave of David Nance to write so openly of his feelings, even though the Civil War had been over for more than forty years. Hundreds of Dallasites, many of them the leaders of the community, had fought with the Confederate forces, or held views strongly opposite to Nance's. Among these was Philip Lindsley, executive editor of the rare historical set.

COL. C. C. SLAUGHTER

Although Dallas was never a cowboy town the way Forth Worth was, it had one of Texas' most important cattlemen as an early citizen. Col. Christopher Columbus

(Lum) Slaughter lived in Dallas from 1870 until his death in 1919. During much of that time, with ownership of banks and three huge West Texas ranches, among other holdings, he was the state's largest individual taxpayer.

Lum Slaughter was born February 9, 1837, in Sabine County and liked to claim that he was the first child born of American parentage in the Republic of Texas. In fact, he was only the first male child born of a marriage that had been contracted under the Republic. At age twelve, he was "making a hand" with cattle on the Sabine River; and while still a teenager, he hauled and sold East Texas lumber in Dallas and bought North Texas wheat in Collin County. Then, using his own ox-treadmill to make much-desired flour from the wheat, he created a $520 nest egg, with which he entered into the cattle business with his father, George W. Slaughter. In 1856 young Lum and his father moved their herd to the raw frontier of Palo Pinto County and began the great Slaughter cattle business.

After the Civil War, Lum successfully trailed herds to the Kansas markets, eventually holding one million acres in Texas ranchlands. In 1871 he began scientific breeding to upgrade Longhorn stock. He created a sensation at one point when he paid five thousand dollars for a prize-winning Hereford bull, Sir Bredwell.

Moving to Dallas in 1870, Slaughter became a successful banker and was the state's greatest Baptist philanthropist, single-handedly saving Baylor University and creating the Dallas sanatorium which is now Baylor Medical Center.

After his first wife, Cynthia Ann Jowell, died in 1876, Slaughter met his second wife, Carrie Averill, while driving cattle through Kansas, where she was teaching school. They were married in 1878 at Emporia, Kansas. In his later years, Slaughter used a specially built Packard automobile to tour his West Texas ranches. A daughter was his driver. The car had a built-in toilet and special luggage space. The Slaughter home in Dallas, where he died in 1919, is the site of a facility at Baylor Medical Center today. Legend has it that, after he had contributed so much money to Baylor University and the Texas Baptist Hospital, the grateful Baptists wished to honor him by naming the hospital for him, but Slaughter good-naturedly pointed out the inappropriateness of using his name for a hospital.

Hiram G. Craig, writing in *Trail Drivers of Texas,* recorded his experiences during a Slaughter ranch roundup.

In about 1883, while working cattle at Snyder, I took a trip west to the
Colorado River and here witnessed the largest "roundup" that I ever saw or
heard speak of. It was the C. C. Slaughter roundup [and] was estimated at

10,000 head of cattle in one herd. These cattle in this roundup were not owned by one individual, but belonged to ranches from a radius of many, many miles, comprising possibly a number of counties. The country was an open range . . . cattle were known to drift as far as 150 miles north. The custom was to have a roundup in the spring of the year and in the fall.

In the Slaughter roundup there were ten chuck wagons and some 90 men. On the evening before the roundup Billy Stanefor, the roundup boss, called for two or three men from each wagon to go out from ten to fifteen miles and make a "dry camp" so that when daylight came each man was ready to bring all the cattle towards the roundup grounds. The men going in different directions, formed a veritable spider's web with the roundup grounds in the center. As soon as the boys would "whoop 'em up" the cattle were on the run and would make for the grounds. The nearer they came to the roundup grounds, the more men would come in sight—forming one big herd.

We found on bringing in these cattle in this manner that five buffalo and twenty or more antelopes had drifted in with the cattle. Several of the boys, I for one, were sure we were going to rope antelopes. We got our loops ready and started for them. Our horses were too short and also a little too slow. We did not rope any antelopes. The roundup being on Slaughter's ranch, the foreman, Gus O. Keith, and his men, including old man Slaughter, cut their beef cattle, cows, and calves first and drove them back on the range to avoid "chousing" them. As soon as Slaughter was through, the next ranch foreman calls out, "No. 1 cut and No. 2 hold," meaning men from wagon No. 1 were to go into the herd and cut all of their cattle while the men of wagon No. 2 held the herd—thus, by two's, to the finish.

LONG DISTANCE TO LANCASTER

Although some Texas historians have assigned the honor to the line between Galveston and Houston, put in operation in 1883, the first successful long-distance telephone line in Texas ran some fifteen miles from Dallas south to Lancaster via Lisbon, and was completed on August 17, 1882.

D. M. Clower, the Civil War telegrapher and pioneer telephone man of the state who had built the Dallas, Fort Worth, Waco, and Austin exchanges, recalled, "On August 2, 1882, at Dallas we started the first extraterritorial [long-distance] line in Texas, the Lancaster, when the town of Lancaster was clamoring for a telephone connection. I was instructed by the company, which was the Southwestern Telegraph and Telephone of Arkansas, to go down there, and if the businessmen of Lancaster would sign a contract guaranteeing $65 per month for two years, we would then connect them to the Dallas Exchange—which was done."

The line was completed on August 17, at which time congratulatory messages were passed back and forth between Mayor W. T. Nance of Lancaster and H. C. Stevenson, secretary of the Dallas Merchants Exchange. Clower noted, "The biggest expense in running the 15-mile line was for poles, which were cut in the Trinity River bottoms and cost $2.50 each, peeled and delivered."

The first telephone exchange in Texas had opened August 21, 1879, in Galveston, and a short time later the Western Union Telegraph Company (using Thomas A. Edison patents) opened the Houston exchange with forty customers. Southwestern Telephone and Telegraph took over in 1881. The Dallas telephone exchange, with forty subscribers, opened June 1, 1881, the Fort Worth exchange on September 1, and Waco on October 1. In 1882, exchanges opened in Brownsville, Brenham, Cleburne, Colorado City, Corsicana, Denison, Gainesville, Greenville, Jefferson, Marshall, Palestine, Paris, Sherman, and Texarkana.

THE VIN-FIZ FLYER

The Vin-Fiz Flyer, a box-kite contraption of an airplane, piloted by Calbraith Perry Rodgers, arrived at Fort Worth on October 17, 1911, during what became the first Atlantic-to-Pacific air flight. Ten thousand spectators turned out for Rodgers's nationally publicized visit, which was sponsored locally by Amon Carter and the *Star-Telegram* newspaper.

The historic Cal Rodgers flight was underwritten by a grape-flavored soft drink named Vin-Fiz, and the craft of that name was a Wright Brothers' E-X type biplane, which "Daredevil Cal" had learned to pilot after only ninety minutes of instruction from the Wrights themselves. Although a large sum had been offered for the first transcontinental flight by a certain date, Rodgers (who was personally wealthy) knew, before his crossing was completed, that he had missed the prize deadline.

The airplane looked and handled like a big box kite, and Rodgers used no compass and no maps on his nation-crossing trip. He followed a special train on the railroads below, but, upon arriving in Texas, he got lost between Denison and Fort Worth, turning down the wrong tracks. While the Fort Worth crowd waited, he found himself over Bonita, in Montague County, where an MKT railroad telegrapher managed to get him word that he was headed in the wrong direction.

On October 18, Rodgers, leaving Fort Worth, detoured to Dallas at the behest of the State Fair of Texas, then in progress, and almost crashed when an eagle tried to attack his flimsy plane over Arlington. From Dallas Rodgers flew to Waco, then continued on a route which passed through San Antonio and El Paso and many towns in between. The Vin-Fiz project inaugurated a very early form of air mail. U.S. postcards, with a special stamp depicting the Vin-Fiz flyer, sold for twenty-five cents each along the way and were posted by the pilot at the next stop. Today they are highly valued philatelic items. One mailed from Waco, the property of a Dallas woman, auctioned for $13,500 in the 1980s.

The entire transcontinental flight was filled with crashes and disasters, but Rodgers finally reached the West Coast forty-nine days out of Brooklyn. He died later in an air crash in California, in 1912. Texas book columnist Judyth Rigler, of San Antonio, explains that, when the plane crashed, pieces of it were used to make a replica of the Vin-Fiz Flyer which hangs in the "Pioneers of Flight" gallery in the National Aviation and Space Museum, part of the Smithsonian Institution in Washington, D.C.

A reader who begs, "for grandpa's sake," that her identity not be given away, writes, "My grandfather used to brag that when he was a young man he saw the 'Vin-Fiz' flyer making the first crossing of the U.S. He was born and raised in Lockhart. Is it possible the 'Vin-Fiz' landed in a place as small as Lockhart?"

The "Vin-Fiz" landed in places smaller than Lockhart but didn't happen to land there. It is possible that grandpa saw Cal Rodgers and his plane at nearby Granger, Austin, or Kyle, where they did land. Here, in addition to the above, are the Texas towns visited by the "Vin-Fiz"—some stops unscheduled: Denison, Whitesboro, Gainesville, Bonita, Fort Worth, Dallas, Waco, San Marcos, San Antonio, LaCoste, Sabinal, Uvalde, Spofford, Del Rio, Sanderson, Alpine, Marfa, Sierra Blanca, Fort Hancock (the military post), and El Paso.

SURVEYING THE PIE

Dallas had some of the earliest, and longest, electric interurban railways in Texas—a major route to Fort Worth began operating in 1902 and another to Denison and Sherman by 1908—but the whole town was eager to go south by rail. Thus, in 1911, it was announced that new interurban lines would be extended south to Waco and intermediate cities, as well as to Corsicana. In the winter of 1911–12, four young men worked surveying the right-of-way for the new Southern Interurban line from Dallas to Waco (later part of the Texas Electric Railway). Helen B. Anthony, in her book, *Lisbon West of the Trinity,* tells of things that happened to some young surveyors at Lisbon, which then was an independent town south of Dallas' Oak Cliff area.

The surveyors—Walter Taylor, Albert (Pete) Cassidy, Sam Epstein, and Edward Meagher—loaded their equipment each morning onto a small wagon and worked their way south along the proposed route. While on the assignment, they lived at George Givens' home in Oak Cliff. Mrs. Givens, a celebrated cook, announced one day, "For you boys' lunch, I've baked a pie." Only three of the surveyors were going to work that particular day, so an argument arose among them about a three-way split of a round pie. None would settle for a crumb less than his share.

They finally agreed that there was only one solution. So the highly accurate survey equipment was brought out and set up in Mrs. Givens' dining room, and the pie, in its uncut glory, was placed in the center of the dining table. There it was surveyed into three precisely equal parts. Work on the projected interurban line got under way just a little late that day as the wagon rolled out of the front yard, but there was no complaint from anyone about getting an unequal slice of Mrs. Givens' superb pie.

Today the motorist driving along U.S. I-35E can often observe, just to the east, the long-abandoned right-of-way they were surveying for the 1911 interurban line.

OVERBECK'S JAIL

The Dallas County jail, back in the 1930s and 1940s, was famous for the food served to inmates—in fact, county officials with enough "rank" often visited the jail just to have a noon bowl of chili. The cook (or cooks—it may have been a secret recipe passed along) was an inmate, and legend says that he wasn't eager to be released because he enjoyed a better home confined to the jail than he might have had living outside.

But long before this, the Dallas jail missed a chance to be unique in all the world, if county leaders had only accepted a proposal from local architect H. A. Overbeck. Overbeck came to Dallas in 1895 and immediately became one of the city's foremost architects. Born in Cincinnati, he had practiced successfully in Omaha prior to opening his Dallas office. He designed some of the most notable structures in Dallas, among them old Saint Paul Hospital; the Linz Building, Dallas' first skyscraper; Dallas University, at Turtle Creek and Oak Lawn; and the MKT Building, which still stands at 701 Commerce. But Overbeck did have his philosophical eccentricities.

He decided to put more than mere ability into the eight-story, fireproof, $600,000 Dallas County Criminal Court and Jail building that he designed in 1913. He declared that he wanted to make it the most humane jail in the nation, constructed for the purpose of treating prisoners like human beings, not captive animals. The jail was to have its own hospital, a modern kitchen on the roof that would supply hot food via dumbwaiters, and any dungeon was to be eliminated.

The Dallas County Commissioners went along with shower baths and an ice-water supply, as well as fans for a pioneer controlled washed-air ventilation system. But they balked when Overbeck declared that his true ambition was to have a pipe organ in the jail that would furnish popular music for recreation and, upon their retiring, sacred music that would "appeal to the prisoners' better natures." He tried to raise pipe-organ money himself, but World War I stopped his campaign for funds. Thus Dallas County missed its historic opportunity to have the only lockup in the world with an official organist.

E . H . R .   G R E E N

Texas has never matched its first multimillionaire and international celebrity, Edward Howland Robinson Green, the six-foot-four, one-legged son of Hetty Green, the "Witch of Wall Street" and the richest woman in America at the time. Her niggardly frugality caused "Ned," as he was called, to lose his leg when he injured it as a boy. She hauled the boy around town, looking for a cut-rate doctor, because she hated to "waste money" on a high-priced doctor for herself or anyone else.

Ned Green came to Texas in 1892 at age twenty-five, to take over the faltering Texas Midland Railway, which his mother gave him. In Terrell, headquarters of the TMR, he deposited $500,000 in a local bank, twice the resources of the bank itself. He entertained pals lavishly and chased women of shady reputations—which cost him his social standing in the little town. But he fooled everyone by being a superb railroad man who helped elevate the rusty Texas Midland to first-class status. He also instituted experimental crops and farms to assist North Texas farmers. At one point he hired the already famous farm expert, Seaman Knapp, to move to Texas and take over his "demonstration" farms. Green's employees adored him, for he was always considerate.

Ned Green brought the first automobile to Texas in 1899, a two-cylinder Saint Louis Gas Car surrey, with a company official sent along to drive him from Terrell to Dallas. Green stayed in Terrell for several years, out of corporate loyalty; but love for Dallas (and nasty Terrell gossip) eventually caused him to move to Dallas, where he built a lavish townhouse so he could live with Mabel, a notorious woman for whom he had named his private railroad car. After his mother's death he married Mabel.

Ned also liked young girls—very young girls—as companions and frequently took a load of them in his private coach for long rail rambles, accompanied by one or another impeccable Dallas couple acting as chaperons. E. J. Kiest, owner of the *Dallas Times Herald,* and his wife frequently were aboard. Several of the girls later were sent to college by Ned Green. He also became the leader of the Texas Republican Party, often operating through Fort Worth's legendary "Gooseneck Bill" McDonald, a black politician.

Ned Green's first car was a phaeton-runabout with a two-cylinder engine, tiller, and buggy top. It cost Green $1,260—more than a year's salary for most Texans. Ned and George Dorris, the designer of the auto, drove it in from Terrell to Dallas on October 5, 1899. They made the thirty-mile trip in five hours—including repair time, when a farm wagon forced the horseless carriage off the road at Forney and damaged it. This must have been Texas' original auto accident, because the *Dallas Times Herald* said that Green's vehicle was the first automobile in the state. Lawsuits were filed against Green after that first trip, based on allegations that his automobile caused horses to run away, wreck buggies, and throw riders in general. (Note: Both Terrell and Forney, Texas, which was on the way, had an automobile operate on their streets before Dallas did.)

Green and Dorris entered Dallas near Fair Park, using what was known as the

East Pike, which closely followed the Texas & Pacific Railway. The horseless carriage made its way down Elm Street to the courthouse, as hundreds of spectators lined the streets. Ned at the time had an apartment in Dallas at Elm and Griffin, so he rode over there and parked the vehicle—but not without a guard.

On his rail rambles (as he called them) Green pulled a special railroad car built to accommodate his chauffeur and his automobile and hooked it on ahead of his private coach on his trips around the United States. As for that first automobile, a story in an October 10, 1910, Dallas newspaper noted that "Old Hurricane" (its nickname) was still in use as a pace car at the State Fair.

MONTGOMERY WARD CAR

Although E. H. R.(Ned) Green's Saint Louis Gas Car is credited with having been the first auto in Texas, there is another automobile, little known to history, that may well share some of that "first auto" credit. Historians Tom Smith and Mike Hazel found this humorous vehicular tale in an 1897 issue of the *Dallas Daily Times Herald:*

The Montgomery, Ward & Co. advertising [railroad] cars arrived in the city this morning and contained among other novelties a horseless carriage, or motorcycle, the first one ever seen on Texas soil. J. Frank Pickering, the manager of [the] advertising car, took several citizens for a "drive" during the afternoon and evening hours and the sight of a carriage moving along with no horses attached created a mild sensation. The carriage is propelled much in the same manner as an electric [street] car except that the power comes from storage batteries, 28 of which are stored away under the seats. It can be backed or turned in any direction and is very easily handled.

Charles Holland and Tom Hammond, city ticket agent for the MKT [Katy] Railroad, and a *Times Herald* man were taken for a drive. Several portions of the city were visited and the ride thoroughly enjoyed. The carriage runs smoothly, and, except for the novelty of having no horses, no difference could be told from that of an ordinary hack ride. An average speed of eight miles an hour is maintained, with a possibility of fourteen. The carriage was moving along at a rapid rate out on Ross Avenue when an old man with long flowing whiskers rushed out of his house and yelled, "Say, I'm going to have you fellers arrested for witchcraft!" Tom Hammond was so charmed with the ride that he is going to buy a few for the Katy to use instead of passenger trains.

Although this automotive curiosity preceded Ned Green's vehicle on the streets of Dallas by some two years, it hardly seems fair to deny Colonel Green first honors. Ned Green's car arrived in October 1899 at Terrell, where it had come by rail, and it remained in Texas. Montgomery, Ward, in contrast, built only two electric cars; and, although they were listed at $3,000 each, they were used solely for advertising and were not for sale. Montgomery, Ward made no more of the electric vehicles. It is interesting to note that Tom Hammond, the Katy Railroad ticket agent, was unwittingly prophetic when he jokingly said he was going to buy a few automobiles to use instead of passenger trains.

SARAH COCKRELL

Sarah Horton came to Dallas with her family in 1844, living on Mountain Creek. The next year she married Alexander Cockrell (called Alec, despite the spelling of his name), even though her family was not convinced that he was a suitable match. He already had a fighter's reputation. Alec Cockrell was a rough-handed freighter, but smart and ambitious. Sarah, who was a plain girl, knew that, with her, he could succeed; and he was tender toward her, if not toward many others. With her help, Alec became a powerful economic figure in early Dallas; he was the entrepreneur who bought out Dallas founder John Neely Bryan's remaining town real estate for a reported seven thousand dollars, a princely sum—although Bryan always said he never made a dollar out of Dallas. Soon Cockrell was owner of a brick plant and the saw mill, and he built the first bridge over the Trinity. He was a man who got things done one way or another. Sarah did his bookkeeping and record keeping, and she taught Alec to write—or at least to sign his name.

The death of Alec Cockrell occurred in 1858, at the height of his Dallas career, after City Marshal Andy Moore arrested Cockrell for being drunk and disorderly. Cockrell paid his fifteen-dollar fine and marched out of the justice of the peace court vowing to fight the marshal. Andy Moore eventually shot Cockrell, after Cockrell went home and armed himself. Was it an ambush or self-defense? One group of historians has viewed Alec Cockrell as a rather dangerous character, one used to handling rough, unruly men and himself stormy, violent, and apt to use his fists or worse. Then, of course, there is a quite different Cockrell family interpretation. A novel about the family and the death of Alec Cockrell, *Destiny in Dallas* by Shirley Seifert, was a 1958 bestseller.

Sarah took over her late husband's business affairs and became Dallas's most successful financier. She assumed control of the various enterprises, having quietly operated them by herself through the years. After the first wooden bridge was washed away (she keeping the ferry franchise), she got a charter from the State of Texas to build an iron bridge over the tumultuous Trinity. It opened in 1872. The stock certificate for the "Dallas Bridge Company" makes no mention of her name. G. W. Swink, the secretary who signed the certificates, also was manager of the first street railway company, where she was also invested. It was not until 1875 that "S. H. Cockrell & Co." was formed, hinting at her ownership; this matter involved Todd Mill, which Sarah had funded and which her son Frank and son-in-law Marshall Gray managed.

Sarah was a noted philanthropist, giving money and land for churches and other beneficial institutions; she even gave money to Constable Moore, a deacon, for construction of the First Methodist Church. By the time of her death in 1892, she owned large quantities of land in the city of Dallas and Dallas County, as well as parcels in Cleburne, Houston, and Mineral Wells. Throughout her business career, whether as owner and a behind-the-scenes director, or as manager of her husband's business, she raised a large family and was much beloved by them and all who knew her. She never became a hardened executive—although always she was a wise and forward-looking one. Her wealth today would run into the hundreds of millions.

The papers of Sarah Horton Cockrell are at the American History Center, University of Texas at Austin. Several historical articles and a biography have been written about her.

The death of Alexander Cockrell has remained one of the more mysterious episodes of early Dallas history. The account offered above is usually taken as correct, but another version, which came later, is contained in the late Joseph M. Wilson's book on the Cockrell family, *Seven Generations in Dallas:*

Nicholas Darnell . . . was employed by a predecessor of the Houston & Texas Central Railroad to negotiate with Alexander Cockrell for right-of-way into Dallas. On the morning of April 3, 1858, negotiations were successfully concluded and Mr. Darnell and Alexander Cockrell had a few drinks to celebrate. They got noisy and Andrew Moore, recently elected town constable [*sic*], arrested Mr. Cockrell and he had to pay a small fine. Moore owed Cockrell money and there had been words between them when the debt went unpaid. Cockrell was unarmed at the time of his arrest [and] he went home and got his five-shooter and double-barreled shotgun and started back uptown. Just as he stepped up onto the southeast corner of Commerce and Broadway [now Dealey Plaza], there was a crash. Moore, hiding in a doorway at the northwest corner of Commerce and Houston, ambushed and shot Mr. Cockrell with a double-barreled 10-gauge shotgun loaded with buckshot. The distance was about 125 feet. Several shots [eight] took effect in the belly, and it was clear that Moore had aimed for a gut shot. Alexander Cockrell was carried home, where he died an hour and a half later.

Andrew Moore was indicted and later acquitted. For a time he was in charge of the old Masonic cemetery near Memorial Auditorium. He died in 1870 and it is thought he was killed by his son, Ernest, in a hunting accident and that Ernest later committed suicide in a fit of remorse over this event.

BIRDMAN OF BIRDVILLE

The story of how a Texas cowboy became a British aviation hero is better known in England than in the place where he was born: the old county seat of Tarrant County, Birdville (now Haltom City).

The flying cowboy was Samuel Franklin Cody, born in 1861, no known kin to "Buffalo Bill" Cody. Samuel Cody spent years ranching in Texas but married an English woman while taking cattle by boat to Great Britain. At times in his career he wrote successful theater pieces and also played with Wild West shows, billed as "Captain Cody, King of the Cowboys." He was a superb rider and was skilled with rope, whip, and rifle.

Sam Cody remained in England for the rest of his life. In 1889, he and his wife Lela Davis formed "The Great Codys" Wild West show and headed for London. A poster in the Fort Worth Museum of Science and History shows a darkly handsome man, with the prescribed poster look of Western entertainers at the time: thick mustaches and goatee and hair falling well below his shoulders. The resemblance to Buffalo Bill is pronounced and probably not accidental.

Sam Cody went up the Chisholm Trail in 1875 and is said to have become interested in kites when a Chinese chuckwagon cook built an unusually large model for him. One of Cody's kites flew fourteen thousand feet high, a world record. Despite success in his shows and stage productions, Cody always dabbled with kites—big, man-lifting kites—that caught the attention of the British navy, which considered using them for aerial reconnaissance at sea. In fact, a ship towed Cody and his man-lifting kite across the English Channel in 1903. A strange, bat-looking kite is part of an award piece given him bearing the inscription, "S. F. Cody, F.RMS. of Texas. U.S.A. Inventor of the famous War Kite." His development of weather kites earned him a fellowship in the Royal Meteorological Society.

He also helped to develop, and then piloted, an airship over a fifty-mile course—one of the most important events in English aviation history. Cody went to work for the British army and showed an intuitive flair for aeronautical design. In 1907, Cody oversaw construction of a powered dirigible and, on October 16, 1908, made the first powered airplane flight in Great Britain in "Army Aeroplane No. 1." In 1909, his wife became the first woman in England to fly as a passenger. He built several airplanes of varied designs.

One year after becoming a British subject, Samuel Cody was killed in 1913, while flight-testing a float plane he planned to use crossing the Atlantic. A large monument at Britain's Farnborough Aviation Center honors the Texan who often is called "Father of British Aviation."

Most information on Samuel Cody's life in the United States may be found in the Special Collections of the library at the University of Texas at Arlington.

GOOSENECK BILL MCDONALD

William Madison (Gooseneck Bill) McDonald was born June 22, 1866, on a farm in Kaufman County, one of eleven children of an Indian mother and an ex-slave father. For forty years he was a force in Texas politics, controlling a block of votes which, though small, could be used to swing the balance of power between battling white factions, especially at presidential conventions. By age thirty-two, he was a Republican kingmaker, a national political force, and the best-known black figure in Texas. His power lay in his ability to help elect the members of the Republican National Committee, who controlled the presidential ticket.

Young Bill persisted for seven years in attending the one-room school in his district, despite its having only a three-month term. A white lawyer named Z. T. Adams tutored him in business and law, made certain he graduated from high school, and, with other Kaufman County residents, supported him in college. (Bill said he walked the seven hundred miles from Kaufman to Nashville, where Roger Williams College—now Fisk University—was located.)

In 1890, living at Forney, he joined the Republican Party, which split into "Lily Whites" and "Black and Tans." One of the half-dozen white members of the Black and Tans was E. H. R. Green, the wealthiest man in Texas; as National Committeemen, he and McDonald controlled the Texas Republican Party for many years. During this period, McDonald became nationally renowned as "Gooseneck Bill" because of his thin neck. Although he lost control of the Texas Republican Party in 1909, he remained politically powerful and was the foremost black financier and real estate developer in the Southwest.

McDonald's genius shone in his organizing of black fraternal and benevolent associations and in his use of the Prince Hall Masons as a force for the political and economic advancement of the black middle class. Even if it meant depleting the treasury of some local lodge, he saw to it that poll taxes were paid and members voted. McDonald died in Fort Worth in 1950.

SOCIALIST SONGSTER

The Rev. Morgan Allen Smith, D.D., born in 1856 in Illinois, at age nineteen journeyed to Texas and later wrote, "I was converted to the Methodist Episcopal Church, South, on July 26, 1876, about sunrise—out in the woods under a post-oak tree, on Peterson's Branch in the western part of Parker County." Next spring he married Lucy Martin, a Methodist minister's daughter. In 1883, he joined the Indian Mission Conference at Eufaula, Indian Territory (now Oklahoma), and remained in Indian Territory for ten years, ministering to several tribes. The Smiths moved back to Texas in 1893, and he became minister at Garland and then Commerce.

Something seems to have changed the Reverend Smith with stunning force, because, within a short time, he had published several Socialist tracts, including "Christ as a Social Reformer" and "Smith's Socialist Songster." In 1911, at Commerce, he published "Socialism in Song," a book using the tunes of old hymns as a framework but offering such inflammatory verses as those below:

BLOODY CAPITALISM
(Washed in the Blood)
Do you cast your ballot so the toiling child
On the altar of greed shall be slain?
In the mills and factories of the idle rich
Shall be murdered for profit and gain?

AMAZING GRAFT
(Amazing Grace)
Amazing graft! how wide its scope
That plunders you and me!
We're now enslaved beneath its yoke
But soon we shall be free.
'Tis graft and greed that rob us all
Of that which we produce.
Until we cease to toil for gain
And create wealth for use.

Rev. Morgan Smith died in Dallas in 1928. His son, Wilford B. ("Pitchfork") Smith, became a well-known Texas political figure, although never so estranged from American politics as his father. But he was no fence-straddler; Pitchfork Smith's publication, *The Pitchfork*, was modeled on W. C. Brann's *The Iconoclast*. Pitchfork Smith died in 1939.

(G. L. Seligmann of the History Department, University of North Texas, compiled the songs above.)

CANADIANS
AT FORT WORTH

In 1916, Canada, already in the Great War in Europe, built three airfields near Fort Worth to train pilots for the Royal Canadian Flying Corps. The Canadian airfields were named Taliaferro, Barron, and Carruthers; they formed a triangle around Fort Worth, with Taliaferro to the north and Barron and Carruthers to the south and southwest. Many American citizens also enlisted in Canadian military units and were assigned to Fort Worth.

Unfortunately, flight instruction was in its infancy and mistakes abounded. Fifty-one pilots were killed flying at the three fields. When the United States entered the war in 1917, the Canadian flying fields were taken over by the Army Air Corps and renamed Hicks, Everman, and Benbrook. Eleven graves of Canadian flyers are marked in Fort Worth's Greenwood Cemetery.

The most celebrated pilot at the Canadian fields was twenty-nine-year-old Capt. Vernon Castle, a native of England, who, with his beautiful young wife Irene, comprised the most sensational dance team in the world. They created such famous ballroom dances as the One-step, the Turkey Trot, the Castle Walk, and the Hesitation Waltz. Born Vernon Blythe in 1887, he was interested in engineering but came to the United States in 1906 with his sister, who was an actress. He took the name Castle in 1907, after he performed a successful dance routine in a Broadway musical (in which his sister got him a small role). Later he became a choreographer as well as a dancer.

Vernon and Irene Foote danced together socially but not as a professional team until after they were married in 1911. The next year they made their sensational dance debut in Paris, to the music of "Alexander's Ragtime Band." Vernon Castle's 1914 book, *Modern Dancing,* became the manual for public ballroom dancing.

The Castles were starring on Broadway in 1916, when Vernon returned to England to enlist in the Royal Flying Corps, eventually winning the Croix de Guerre in France for one hundred missions over enemy lines. He was sent to Fort Worth at the beginning of 1918 to instruct air cadets at Carruthers Field, near present Benbrook. The Castles were cordial but quite elegant, driving a Rolls-Royce and living in Fort Worth's fashionable Westbrook Hotel. They proved to be delightful social assets to Fort Worth, Dallas, and surrounding towns, where everyone was eager to entertain these international celebrities. Their Rolls was to be driven and maintained by Ely Green of Waxahachie, a young black man whom Captain Castle met, who was not only a chauffeur but also a mechanic.

Captain Castle was killed on February 15, 1918, when, to avoid colliding with a student pilot, he was forced to put his plane into a steep climb too near the ground and it crashed. Ely was driving in the airfield gate to meet Vernon Castle for his first day on the job when an ambulance came tearing by, and he said he sensed that something terrible had happened. (Ely Green told about it many years later in a book he wrote, *Too Black, Too White.*)

Irene Castle, sometimes credited with starting the "bobbed hair" craze in the 1920s, retained her Castle name and her fame as a fashion trendsetter through subsequent marriages. She was devoted to protection of animals and founded the Orphans of the Storm animal shelters in 1928. She died in 1969. A popular movie of their marriage was titled *The Story of Vernon and Irene Castle.*

WICHITA TRUCKS

Of the independent motor vehicles manufactured in Texas, none was as successful as the Wichita truck, built by the Wichita Falls Motor Company in that North Texas city from 1911 to 1932. The firm was established by Joseph A. Kemp and owned with his brother-in-law, Frank Kell, both natives of Clifton, Texas, and both important railroad and milling investors and Wichita Falls philanthropists.

The Wichita Falls Motor Company made only trucks. (Another motor company made the "Wichita Combination Car" for one year, 1920–21.) Wichita trucks gained a reputation for rugged strength and were used, wisely, in the Texas, Oklahoma, Arkansas, and California oil and lumbering industries. By 1918, the firm was building several kinds and sizes of trucks. The one-ton Model A was a chain-drive vehicle with solid rubber tires, which sold for $1,800. Model K was the same truck with worm-drive. The Model B Wichita truck was a two-ton chain-drive which sold for $2,500 and probably was the most popular vehicle the firm made. The Model M was the same truck in worm-drive. Other sizes went from 2-1/2 and 3-1/2 tons to Model Q, a five-ton worm-drive monster which sold for $4,300. Despite a note that "We do not claim to manufacture anything designed for this particular class of work," Model Q was advertised as "A special designed truck for log or lumber transportation." Added was the claim: "This truck moved as many logs in 9 hours as 24 mules did in 10 hours on a haul of 12 miles." The company's house organ was titled *Wichitauk*. Factory branch offices and service stations were maintained in San Francisco, Los Angeles, San Antonio, Houston, New Orleans, and Dallas.

Wichita trucks were big, square vehicles. For many years the steering wheel was located in the center or on the right-hand side. Early models had to be cranked to start but were famed for the ease with which they cranked—this at a time when Model T Fords were notorious for "kicking" and breaking arms with the crank handle. The Wichita Falls Motor Company at one time claimed it had ten thousand trucks operating in eighty-seven different countries. The company also made fire trucks. One, made in 1912 for the Seguin Fire Department, is operational and on display at the Fireman's Museum of Texas at Grand Prairie.

The Wichita truck firm closed when the Depression hit and Kemp died. Surviving examples are few and bring big prices at collector auctions.

ARLINGTON DOWNS

For a few years in the 1930s, the Dallas–Fort Worth area had one of the finest horse tracks in the nation: Arlington Downs, north of the city of Arlington along the Bankhead Highway (now U.S. 80). Built by oilman and rancher W. T. Waggoner (the only son of Decatur's pioneer cattle king, Dan Waggoner), the track featured the Waggoner brand—three reversed Ds in a pyramid—on everything from stock to clubhouse to oil tanks.

W. T. Waggoner began construction of the racing plant in 1930 on his beautiful Three D Stock Farm, which was already a North Texas showplace for horses. He planned the track more from love of horses, he said, than from love of gambling. The first couple of years, races were run with only friendly wagering, but in 1933, when Texas legalized pari-mutuel betting, Waggoner spent millions on a covered grandstand for eight thousand spectators, a sumptuous brick clubhouse adjoining it, and the landscaped track circling an artificial lake.

Crowds poured in for the spring and fall meets, but success was Arlington Downs' downfall, opening as it did in the depths of the Depression. North Texas merchants joined the churches in a crusade against gambling, claiming absenteeism from work and worship, as well as disastrous credit losses. By 1936, pari-mutuel betting was outlawed. An even greater blow to Arlington Downs, however, had been the death, late in 1934, of Col. W. T. Waggoner.

For years Arlington Downs was preserved but used only for an occasional auto race. In World War II, it became a military vehicle park. In the 1950s, a portion of the Three D Stock Farm became the site of a General Motors assembly plant. A reminder of the 1930s experiment is a remaining name: Arlington Downs Road.

THE DALLAS
FORD PLANT

In 1909, the Ford Motor Company opened a two-man service center in Dallas to take care of its recently introduced Model T. By 1914, the demand for Model Ts was so great that Ford opened a Dallas assembly plant in the 1900 block of Main and Commerce, with a capacity of 150 cars per day.

This downtown location never was handy, and in 1925 a new plant was dedicated on East Grand, along the Texas & Pacific Railway, embracing twenty-three acres, with a main building 300 by 840 feet. For years, Dallas motorists joked that the assembly line was located near White Rock Creek so that wooden-spoke wheels could be kept tight by soaking them in the creek.

In the mid-thirties, the Dallas assembly plant experienced a good many of the labor problems that the auto industry underwent across the United States. Union organizers reportedly were beaten and tarred and feathered. Dallas newspapers carried stories of labor troubles almost daily for a lengthy period. The introduction of the "Ford V-8" engine was celebrated in Dallas like a holiday, so important was this new development to the Ford plant and Ford's future. Toward the end of the 1930s, the Dallas plant began putting oval stickers in the rear windows of the cars coming off the line which read, "Built in Texas by Texas Labor." This was reportedly done at the suggestion of a local city official, who said the well-known loyalty of Texans for their state would cause sales to increase if Lone Star customers knew their Ford had been built by fellow Texans. This slogan was amended to read "Built in Texas by Texans" and became nationally renowned—and the basis, worldwide, for hundreds of joking parodies, many a trifle off-color.

During World War II, over 100,000 Jeeps and military trucks were assembled by the Dallas plant. In 1947, the one-millionth Texas Ford automobile was produced. But the plant layout became obsolete, and on February 28, 1970, the last Ford "Built in Texas by Texans" rolled off the line, and the Dallas Ford assembly plant was closed.

Dale S. Campbell of Dallas recalled trying to do business with the 1914 Ford Motor Company assembly plant:

> Other automobile companies had show rooms in the business area but if you wanted to buy a Ford you had to go to the factory. I was a student at Southern Methodist University in 1916, and my father sent me down to buy a car. I had a check for the full price, $424.10, as the only way you could buy a car was for cash. We lived at 3515 Crescent, so I had to walk to Knox Street and get a streetcar to the plant.
>
> When the car came off the assembly line they asked me if I could drive and I said, yes, and asked was it ready to go? They said, yes, it was ready; it had oil but it needed some gasoline. I asked if they would furnish enough gasoline for me to get home as I only lived three or four miles away. They said, no, so I said, "Give me my check back and I will go buy an Overland."
>
> They gave me my check back and I went home on the streetcar, but before I got there they had called my father and told him to send that boy back, they would give him some gasoline. I went back and got the car, with gasoline, and drove it all my school years.

TEXAS PRESIDENT
OF BROOKLYN

A Texan was once the president of Brooklyn. He was Martin W. Littleton, born in Tennessee, who had come with his family to Parker County, west of Fort Worth, at age nine. His family returned to Tennessee when Martin was sixteen, but he refused to leave Texas and supported himself in Weatherford as a printer's devil and a track walker on the Texas & Pacific Railway, which ran east-west across the county.

One Saturday afternoon, before a gathering of farmers and townspeople in a Weatherford store, young Littleton recited an oration (reportedly while standing on a barrel-head) and was told by one of the crowd that he sounded just like a New York lawyer. This inspired young Martin to be a lawyer, although he hadn't read a word of law or received much education—and, for that matter, was pretty sure the listener hadn't actually heard a New York lawyer.

Littleton managed to attend nearby Springtown Academy for six months, then talked lawyer S. W. T. Lanham of Weatherford (who later became governor of Texas) into letting him read law in his office. In 1891, Littleton was admitted to the bar—at the tender age of nineteen.

He moved to Dallas and in 1893 became prosecuting attorney of Dallas County. On December 31, 1896, he married Maude Wilson, the only girl he ever courted. But he warned her that he planned to be a New York lawyer, and in 1897 they left Dallas for the big city, with one thousand dollars in borrowed money and a letter of recommendation from a Dallas judge.

Littleton's professional rise in New York was rapid. After serving as district attorney of Kings County, in 1904 he became president of the Borough of Brooklyn—and Dallas gave a celebration dinner in his honor when he returned for a visit. In 1908 he successfully defended Harry K. Thaw in the murder of Stanford White (part of the "Girl in the Velvet Swing" episode). From 1910 to 1913, Littleton was a New York congressman. He died in 1934.

The
State
of Central
Texas

CENTRAL TEXAS

Of the five states of Texas, "Central Texas" is the most inadequately designated. As you might expect, its boundaries mostly depend on where the assumed lines of the other four states are drawn. Does this mean there is something artificial about the "state" of Central Texas? Absolutely not. Hillsboro marks a northern border, and the area from Waco to Austin is the Main Street of our Central Texas state. And, as is true of other "states," there are a number of governmental organizations and commercial enterprises carrying "Central Texas" in their name.

So, where are the elusive "Central Texas" boundaries? To begin with, Central Texas is not the exact center of the Lone Star State. The geographical center of Texas is just a few miles out of Brady, in McCulloch County—but Bradyites don't often think of their town as being in Central Texas. On the other hand, San Antonio would seem to be in the "state" of Central Texas, but virtually everybody in Texas thinks of San Antonio as being part of South Texas. And San Marcos, between Austin and San Antonio, is the home of Southwest Texas State University.

Just for purposes of definition, here are some of the western border towns of Central Texas: Clifton, Hamilton and Lampasas. The Temple–Belton–Killeen–Fort Hood area is the heart of Central Texas. On the eastern edge, there is the problem of Bryan and College Station: Central Texas or East Texas? And should Corsicana, Mexia, and Groesbeck be part of Central Texas? Or Calvert, Giddings, Lockhart, and La Grange? Regardless, these towns make good regional markers for Central Texas.

Of course, as is true of the Gulf Coast and the farther reaches of West Texas, there is a state-within-a-state that goes along with Central Texas; that's the Hill Country. Although parts of the Hill Country extend or intrude on other sections, it carries its own definition; when speaking to a Texan, you can merely refer to "the Hill Country" without adding further geographical description (to some extent, this applies to the larger geological region of the Edwards Plateau). Already enriched by its Germanic past, the Hill Country has become a prime natural retreat, where deer stands and cabins, used during the hunting seasons, are maintained by families from all over Texas, continuing in such use for three, even four generations.

Regardless of its imprecise boundaries, the character of Central Texas, the "state" itself, is shaped by its surroundings. It is central to the rest of Texas in many more ways than geographically. Austin, which every year assumes extra historical magnetism because it is the state capital, has immense political and educational investments. Today it more and more frequently assumes leadership in such things as Texas' "national" music and its amateur theater. Austin is generally accepted as the place where more Texans would like to live than any other spot. It also has a long reputation for liberal political activities, less in the Texas legislature than in Austin city politics.

However, such liberalism is not representative of the rest of Central Texas. In general, the towns and cities of the "state" of Central Texas are quite conservative, not only in their politics but in their culture and development. Central Texans tend to retain their rugged individualism. "You can't tell me what to do," could be the motto of any number of people and places in Central Texas. Parts of Central Texas are, more and more often, becoming the retirement regions of choice— not just such famous Hill Country places as Wimberly and Fredericksburg, but towns like Lampasas, Hamilton, and Salado. Part of what draws retirement residents is the history and the well-preserved nineteenth- and early-twentieth-century houses and other structures still available to add color and interest to the towns. But history can't always stand up to what some residents see as progress, and much of the historical character of Central Texas is being abandoned or destroyed. Traffic on Interstate Highway 35, which extends through the center of Central Texas from north to south, is changing the character of the areas immediately adjoining this international roadway from Canada to Mexico.

There is thriving growth in many parts of Central Texas, as in the Fort Hood–Killeen–Temple–Belton area and the northern and eastern suburbs of Austin, such as Round Rock and Georgetown. The resort and park areas around the many lakes are home to thousands of retirees and other kinds of permanent residents. But Central Texas, like parts of East Texas, is dotted with old lost cotton towns, left abandoned as cotton moved to the High Plains; a few county seats cling to the courthouse for survival. Drive off the main highways, and you can find the magnificent residences (or their shells) of the cotton kings and nineteenth-century bankers, the former business sections lined with empty banks, department stores, hotels, even hospitals; these towns are haunted by memories of the success of the first half of the twentieth century and the failure of the second. The last reminder of the grandeur of this agricultural past may be an ornate First Baptist or First Methodist church building, the only present grandeur a consolidated high school with a well-lighted football field.

MORMONS IN TEXAS

In November 1845, some 150 Mormons under the leadership of Lyman Wight, aged forty-nine, entered Texas at the Red River town of Preston, convinced that Texas was the new Zion. Wight had suffered greatly while living in Missouri. There he and several other Mormon leaders were accused of treason but were allowed to escape to Illinois. Wight was a member of the Quorum of Twelve Apostles of the Mormon Church, and he considered himself second in command after the death, at the hands of an Illinois mob, of Joseph Smith the Prophet, founder of Mormonism. Wight refused to accept Brigham Young's leadership, leaving Young's Utah-bound group to lead his own group to Texas, claiming that Joseph Smith, before his death, had ordered him to do so.

The Mormon band contained several trained artisans, and it is believed that they helped construct Glen Eden, the elegant log home of Holland and Sophia Coffee, the largest log structure in Texas. The Mormons remained in Grayson County at a site that became known as Mormon Grove. In the summer of 1846, the Mormons followed the Preston Road south, crossing the Trinity River at Cedar Springs, a settlement two miles north of the village of Dallas. They settled near Austin, on the Colorado River, getting a contract to build the first Travis County jail, as well as constructing the first mill on the Colorado, at the present site of Tom Miller Dam. The Mormons were well received. Noah Smithwick, in *Evolution of a State,* recalls, "Curious to know something of their peculiar views, I permitted the Elder (Wight) to preach in my house."

The Colorado River mill proved to be too exposed to floods, and the group moved to the Pedernales River, some four miles southeast of Fredericksburg, building another mill and creating a community named Zodiac. Wight became the second (actually the first to serve) chief justice of Gillespie County—occupying the position now called county judge. But by 1850, that mill, too, was washed away. Smithwick says Wight claimed that, through a dream, he was able to recover the millstones. In 1851, a beautiful spot on Hamilton Creek, eight miles south of Burnet, was chosen, becoming known as Mormon Mill Colony, with a furniture factory as well as a grist mill. But the colony soon was deeply in debt, and Mormon Mill was sold to Smithwick in 1853. This time the Mormons settled on the Medina River near Bandera, moving, in 1854, twelve miles downriver to Mountain Valley (now covered by Medina Lake). Lyman Wight conducted the first marriage in Bandera County, uniting one of his sons with a Mormon girl.

Wight had a powerful personality, being called "The Wild Ram of the Mountains" because of his determined leadership. In 1858 he said he had a premonition that there would be war between the slaveholding states and the North. He was greatly opposed to slavery and ordered his band northward. On the second day of the journey, near San Antonio, Wight died unexpectedly. He was buried in the Mormon cemetery at Rocky Hill (Zodiac). As all business was done and all property held in his name, his death caused the Mormons to divide into several groups. A few, including three Wight sons, remained in Texas, but the majority of the Mormons went to Galland's Grove, Iowa, a landmark move in the history of the Reorganized Mormon Church. Wight's three sons in Texas fought for the Confederacy during the Civil War.

Wight today is honored as one of the most important of the founding Saints. A large monument in his honor was raised in Iowa.

SALADO COLLEGE

In the nineteenth century, there were dozens of so-called colleges scattered across Texas, most of them located in small towns because big cities were considered dens of iniquity and the colleges were almost all church-connected. Salado College, at the Bell County town of the same name, was the first in the state to be operated without denominational or state ties.

On October 8, 1859, a tent meeting was held at the Salado Springs, near the present Stagecoach Inn, and the "Salado College Joint Stock Company" was organized. Col. Elijah S. C. Robertson donated one hundred acres of land including two large springs located on Salado Creek. Some five thousand dollars' worth of stock was subscribed, and the company was incorporated by a special act of the Texas Legislature on February 12, 1860. The articles of association in the charter of the school stipulated that the college should never become sectarian, nor should "the peculiar doctrines of any religious denomination be taught therein."

A temporary wooden building was erected, in which a primary school was opened on February 20, 1860, with the Rev. Levi Tenney, a Presbyterian minister, as principal. (His home still stands.) On July 4, 1860, the cornerstone was laid for a large two-story building to house the college. The larger college tract was laid out in blocks, lots, and streets, and the village of Salado grew rapidly.

In July 1861, Dr. J. H. Anderson became college president. A special act of the legislature in 1866 made the sale or gift of intoxicating liquor within six miles of the college a misdemeanor. A later attempt to open a saloon in the town of Salado, less than a mile from the college itself, was thwarted by women who sat in the saloon, challenging husbands or male friends to drink. Not daring to evict the ladies physically, the saloon proprietor closed his saloon after one day.

Salado College was educational home to several well-known Texans, including Texas Gov. Miriam A. (Ma) Ferguson. Her husband, Governor Jim, whose father was a miller on Salado Creek, also attended for a short period. By 1882, however, colleges were closing in the smaller towns, prompted by the growing number of State of Texas schools drawing students to these larger colleges. Salado College's magnificent stone building became a high school for a period, but the site was abandoned after a series of three suspicious fires destroyed the structure. The basis for this arson seems lost in village legend. The one-day saloon still stands, and the remaining stones of the college form a historic brow for College Hill. A larger-than-life bronze statue of Colonel Robertson, sword in hand, now stands looking over the town and guarding the ruins of Salado College.

FIRST WAR
CORRESPONDENT

George W. Kendall, Texas' first war correspondent, found that being a noncombatant reporter was unsafe. In 1841, correspondent Kendall, in bad health and looking for story material, joined the Texas Santa Fe expedition, representing the *New Orleans Picayune,* which he had founded in 1837. He spent two years in prison when what purported to be a trading expedition was captured in New Mexico by Mexican authorities and marched to Mexico City. Much of Kendall's prison time was spent in Mexico's infamous Perote castle. His *Narrative of the Texas Santa Fe Expedition,* published in 1844, remains the best account of that fateful expedition and is considered one of the finest campaign narratives ever written—although J. Frank Dobie criticized it as "journalistically verbose." It was successful as a book, going through seven editions by 1856, and it remains in print today.

During the Mexican-American War, George Kendall gained fame as the first modern war correspondent, with front-line stories written while riding with Ben McCulloch's Texas Rangers and as aide-de-camp to U.S. Gen. William Worth (for whom Fort Worth was named). Kendall, in another original move, sent his dispatches to the *Picayune* by pony express. In 1851, he wrote *The War Between the United States and Mexico, Illustrated,* which a bibliographer said contained "the very best American battle scenes in existence."

Although given a land grant by Texas President Anson Jones in 1841, the New Orleans journalist did not become a Texas resident until after 1848, settling near New Braunfels, where he wrote his Mexican War book. In Paris to arrange the artwork for his portfolio, he met Adeline de Valcourt (1830–1924), who was beautiful (as early photographs prove), cultivated, and strong. They were married in Antwerp and became parents of two sons and two daughters—all born in Europe, because the Kendalls' marriage was kept secret for years.

In 1857, George Kendall bought Post Oak Springs Ranch in what is now Kendall County (named for him) and raised sheep and goats, experimenting with pedigreed sheep so that he earned the title of "father of the sheep business in Texas." A native of New Hampshire (born in 1807), he was not an active participant in the Civil War but took the Confederate oath of allegiance in order to continue to do business—and to survive.

Kendall died in 1867, in debt, and his wife Adeline took over management of their ranches, showing great executive ability. She was remarried, to Benjamin F. Dane, the ranch manager. The first daughter, Georgina Kendall Fellowes (1850–1947), became a family historian and archivist; she is fondly remembered in San Antonio, where she was active in all aspects of cultural life. The voluminous Kendall Archives was researched by rare book dealer Dorothy Sloan and her husband in 1989, and much new Kendall history was discovered.

AUSTIN IN THE RECONSTRUCTION ERA

The Reconstruction period in Texas, after the Civil War, often is portrayed as a time of tribulation for the state, but Austin is an example of a city that accepted Reconstruction without much turmoil.

In 1861, Travis County, with Austin as its seat, had voted against secession 704 to 450, and some of the state's leading Unionists remained in Austin throughout the war. Capt. Hubbard Carrington's "Austin Company" of the federal army fought in the "last battle of the Civil War" at Palmito Ranch, Texas, on May 13, 1865. When the first bluecoats arrived in Austin on July 25, 1865, they met not opposition but a rally, at Congress Avenue and Pecan (now West Sixth) Street. And, on August 2, when A. J. Hamilton, a former Austin resident and federal army leader, was appointed governor of Texas, one historian who was there recorded that "a large concourse assembled . . . met Hamilton at his home, two miles east of town, and escorted him into the city and to the capitol." Maj. Gen. George Armstrong Custer and his wife Libbie spent some pleasant months in Austin in 1866–67, being well received by the townspeople, as she recorded in her classic volume, *Tenting on the Plains.*

Acrimony toward the freedmen was not as evident in Austin as it was in most parts of Texas. When the first Negro school opened in 1868, a black children's march to the new schoolhouse was staged down Congress Avenue, and the white population, watching from the curb, "seemed to regard the affair with favor," according to one newspaper. Another editorialist drew a picture of daily life: "Saturday in Austin—In passing . . . we hear German, Swedish, Spanish and rich brogue. The shops are thronged with eager customers. Another feature is the free intermingling of colors without misunderstanding. Snowy white and sooty pass and repass without collision."

Even the regime of Republican Gov. E. J. Davis, considered the worst of all Texas Reconstruction administrations, didn't bother Austin; Austin knew him. He, too, had been a resident before the war, having lived there since he was a boy.

By March 1870, Texas was readmitted to the Union and the "ironclad oath," barring most former Confederates from voting, was repealed. In January 1874, the final month of Reconstruction in Texas, tension was at its peak. Governor Davis literally refused to yield the office to Richard Coke, a Democrat, who had outpolled him. Both factions had armed men standing by, but no blood was shed, and E. J. Davis left the capitol on the morning of January 19 without further resistance. He lived out his days as a prosperous Austin lawyer. His homestead was on the Colorado River, where an elegant hotel now stands.

ROBERT T. HILL

In 1874, at age fifteen, Robert Thomas Hill came to Comanche, Texas, from Tennessee and began work as a printer on the local newspaper, the *Chief.* Wondering how seashells got into the strata on nearby Round Mountain, more than three hundred miles from the sea, he acquired a copy of James D. Dana's *Textbook of Geology*. He found, however, that the fossils around Comanche were different from any pictured in the book. After several trips across the peculiar physiography of West Texas, Hill enrolled in 1882 in Cornell University, taking along a trunk full of rocks rather than clothes.

Although without formal preparation for college work, Hill was able to take graduate courses, and his graduation thesis, "Present Condition of Knowledge of the Geology of Texas," was published by the United States Geological Survey. Hill's first field paper, concerning the geology of the Texas Cross Timbers, initially was declined by the *American Journal of Science* as being too revolutionary, but a visit by Hill with the editor, Professor Dana of the geology text, did the trick.

In the mid-1880s, Hill became part of the remarkable scientific coterie of Maj. J. W. Powell, the Western explorer, geologist, and ethnologist who laid the foundations of the U.S. Geological Survey and the Bureau of Ethnology. As assistant professor of geology at the University of Texas and with the State Geological Survey, Hill began studies of the Texas Cretaceous, which brought him international fame. His work and writings covered areas from California to Panama (he is called "Father of Antillean and Isthmian Geology") and dealt with topics as diverse as artesian water, desert environments, paleontology, Indian life, Texas history, metallic resources, habitats of prehistoric peoples, ore deposits, climatology, and petroleum geology. Hill coined many now-familiar Texas geological and geographical terms, including Balcones Escarpment, Edwards Plateau, Woodbine Sand(stone), Trans-Pecos, Lampasas Cut-Plain, Central Denuded Region, and the Gypsum Plains. He died in Dallas in 1941, and his ashes were scattered over Round Mountain, where his geological quest began.

CARPETBAGGERS AND SCALAWAGS

In the Reconstruction period following the Civil War, *carpetbaggers* was a term referring to northern opportunists who stuck everything they owned in a carpet-bag (a cheap suitcase made from carpet remnants) and hurried down to scavenge the occupied South. *Scalawags* was the name applied to southerners who cooperated with the federal government. Several southern states did have a period of extreme "carpetbag rule," which implied legislative control by uneducated former slaves and imported "activists." This was not the case in Texas, although some Texas historians have referred to "the carpetbag yoke" or "Texas under carpet-bagger rule."

There was only one influential "carpetbagger" in Texas Reconstruction government: G. T. Ruby, a Negro journalist and educator who had gone to Louisiana from Maine in 1864 to set up schools for the blacks after the federal capture of New Orleans. Ruby came to Texas in 1866 to continue his school work and served as a member of the Constitutional Convention of 1869. He represented the Galveston district as senator in the 12th and 13th Texas Legislatures before returning to New Orleans in 1873. He is credited with contributions to public school policy and to Galveston's economic recovery.

Texas "scalawags" were anything but "strangers and traitors," as one editor scornfully called them. A. J. Hamilton, a Unionist who was appointed first post-war governor in 1865, had been attorney general and U.S. congressman from Texas before the Civil War. J. W. Throckmorton, elected in 1866 to succeed Hamilton, was one of the eight Secession Convention delegates who voted against Texas leaving the Union, although he had become a Confederate general. As Texas' Indian commissioner during the Civil War, he had been given the nickname "Old Leathercoat." E. M. Pease, appointed governor in 1867 to replace Throckmorton, had fought in the Texas Revolution and was twice elected governor in the 1850s. He and his family were among the most popular members of Austin society.

Edmund J. Davis, historically viewed as the most hated of the Reconstruction governors (actually, Reconstruction had ended), was a Florida native who had lived in Texas since age eleven and had been active in South Texas law and politics before the Civil War. The fact that he had raised federal troops in Texas and fought Confederate forces created much of the enmity felt toward him. Despite his reputation, however, Davis remained honored and well-liked in Austin until his death in 1883.

WOOTAN WELLS

In 1879, in an age when spas were fashionable, a well dug in the northwestern corner of Robertson County proved to be highly mineralized—analysis of the water showed it to contain sulphuric acid, chlorides, magnesia, lime, and oxides of iron, alumina, and manganese.

Within months, the Wootan Wells health resort had arisen at the well, some three miles southwest of Bremond. The resort was planned and laid out by the Wootan Wells Company, of F. M. Wootan, Richard and T. M. Wade, and William M. McKinnie. The company owned the town's four mineral wells, three more having been drilled. According to the *Texas Gazetteer* of 1884–85, by 1883 Wootan Wells could boast the "excellent" Wootan Wells Hotel, managed by Judge Jones J. Kendrick, Mrs. Mary C. Dillard's Avenue Hotel, Mrs. James R. Simmons's Simmons House, and Mrs. James A. Walker's hotel, as well as James Walker's saloon (called "Well #5") and billiard parlor, John Walker's restaurant, Alonzo C. Walker's bathhouse, Evel E. Walker's barbershop, and Percy W. Walker's shooting gallery and skating rink. Dances were held twice weekly at the elaborate pavilion, with its Mexican string-band—and the nights glowed with romantic gaslights along the streets.

In addition to the more elaborate hotels and entertainment centers, the resort contained James A. Carson's general store, Dr. James M. Willis's drug store, James Jackson's meat market, and Ben Test and Ed McGlaun's cotton gin. There was a gun club for members only, two grist mills, and a livery and boarding stable operated by John Simmons. One convenience few other spas in Texas could boast was the narrow-gauge street railway, powered by mules, which went two miles from a stop on the Houston & Texas Central Railroad to the resort's "Cottage Row" and hotel loop, advertised as "conveying passengers from the depot at all hours of the day."

Fires plagued Wootan Wells in the late eighties, and in 1891 hot mineral water was discovered at nearby Marlin, which advertised, "Hottest Water in Texas." By 1900, Marlin had drawn off most of Wootan Wells's visitors and many residents. In 1915 a fire, said to have been started by someone burning out a wasps' nest, destroyed the Wootan Wells Hotel and much of the remaining town. A bottling plant burned in 1921 (the water originally was put up in antique "pop-top" bottles which were opened by a blow from the palm), and after 1923 the town disappeared.

THE CANNING
OF CHACON

William Leslie Black was an imaginative figure in Texas history who had his share of adventure before becoming a Texan. Born in New Orleans in 1843, he joined the Confederate army in 1862 and was wounded at Shiloh. He became a blockade runner and was captured by Union forces but released when he convinced his captors that he was a British subject (his parents were Scotch and English). In 1864 he joined an expedition to capture federal vessels along the Central American Pacific coast but was captured and imprisoned at Alcatraz. Although sentenced to hang for piracy, he kept the prison's books and was pardoned. Following the Civil War he worked in New York in oil, tobacco, and cotton. In 1871, he became a charter member of the New York Cotton Exchange and later was vice-president of the Saint Louis Cotton Exchange.

Colonel Black bought fifty sections of Texas ranch land (32,000 acres) at ten cents per acre, later acquiring some 50,000 acres more around the headwaters of the San Saba River in western Menard County and naming it "Rancho Escondido." When cattle did not prosper because of the nature of the land, he turned to raising sheep and goats, starting with 7,000 head and soon shipping 15,000 goats northward.

As there was no local market, he decided to begin a goat-meat cannery at his homestead overlooking Fort McKavett, adding a tannery later. In 1893, he canned the meat of 3,000 goats and in 1894 the meat of 4,000. He built a model community, with small houses and a store, for his employees. He attempted to open a Wool Exchange, but eastern opposition stalled the project for forty-one years. Colonel Black never gave up on his belief in all phases of goat raising, and in 1900 he authored *A New Industry; or, Raising Angora Goats for Profit*. At one point, goat raisers, supporting the cannery idea, attempted to "sell" the idea of goat meat to Texas appetites by renaming it *chacon*.

William Leslie Black died in 1931 and is buried at his ranch near Fort McKavett. The few labels surviving from his chacon canning industry are much sought after by historians and other collectors.

BLIND MAN'S TOWN: ADAM JOHNSON

Marble Falls, on the Colorado River in Burnet County, for years was called "The Blind Man's Town" because founder Adam Rankin Johnson, who had been blinded in the Civil War, planned and laid out his town from memory.

Adam Johnson had come to Texas from Kentucky in 1854, at age twenty, and become fascinated with the idea of harnessing the Colorado River to power future factories and mills on its banks. He chose Shirley Shoals, west of Burnet, for the site of a future dam. He became Burnet County's first surveyor and worked in West Texas, going northward to the site of Buffalo Gap in modern Taylor County and then far west to the Pecos River, well before civilization got there.

Johnson married Josephine Eastland in 1861, then joined the Confederate army in Kentucky, rising to brigadier general through his guerrilla activities along the Ohio River. At one engagement he bluffed a larger Union army with two stovepipes mounted on wheels, convincing the enemy that he had sufficient artillery. Subsequently he was nicknamed "Stovepipe."

Late in the war, while leading a charge, he was accidentally hit by one of his own men. He was left by his troops in hopes that he would be captured and that federal surgeons could save his life. They did save his life, but not his eyesight. (So certain of his death had his troops been that many southern newspapers carried his obituary fifty-eight years early.)

After the war, the blind General Johnson returned to Burnet, where he opened a successful land office and in 1884 built a home called "Airy Mount" (still standing). With a young son as driver, he directed his buggy to various spots, guided by memory. This motivated him, in 1887, to create the town of Marble Falls, where he envisioned a huge cotton mill utilizing local crops. He obtained financing for the cotton factory and laid out a water system and hydraulic power plant—only to have the latter washed out by one of the Colorado's periodic floods. In rebuilding, Johnson insisted on granite walls tapering from six feet at the base to thirty inches at the top. By donating seven miles of right-of-way, he obtained the railroad that hauled granite from nearby Granite Mountain for the new Texas State Capitol building. Johnson and Dallas financier C. H. Alexander started a dam on the Colorado, but it was abandoned before completion. Only in the 1950s was the Marble Falls dam built.

Adam Rankin Johnson died in 1922, but "The Blind Man's Town" remains one of Texas' favorite recreation centers.

THE "HELLO SUCKER!" GIRL

Mary Louise Cecilia Guinan was Waco's most colorful hometown girl. Although called "Mayme" by her family, she became known as "Texas" once she went on the stage. She gained great notoriety as a Prohibition-era New York nightclub hostess who fronted for various mob investors, but she was immensely popular with the media because of her antics. The best known of these was her habit of saluting her speakeasy customers—many of them sports stars and underworld figures—with "Hello, Sucker!" She once confided, after her speakeasy days, that she was so frightened the first few months on her job, that her supposedly sarcastic greeting was more often aimed at herself than it was at the famous tough guys coming in the door.

Born on Jan. 24, 1884, one of seven children, she was baptized the next day at the Catholic Saint Mary's Church of the Assumption in Waco. Her father was a partner in a wholesale grocery business. She renamed herself "Mayme" in the years she attended Sacred Heart convent in what is now downtown Waco. As a girl she was notorious for playing pranks, once getting spanked hard for setting out with a baby in a tub on the swollen Brazos River. When her father Mike's grocery firm went bankrupt in 1902, the family moved to Denver; and it was there, while still in school, that she was offered an understudy's job with a traveling theater group out of New York. She eventually acted in vaudeville and with the Schuberts, then made several silent Westerns in Hollywood. The best-known pictures of "Texas" show her in cowboy gear—and display her pixie charm and good looks.

Early in the 1920s, as Prohibition prevailed, she became involved with the underworld, although her personal reputation remained high. She was the most famous speakeasy owner in New York, "a boisterous blonde who presided over a whole series of rowdy places," as Time-Life Books' *This Fabulous Century* described her. When one club was shut down, she simply moved to another. Friends testified that she never touched liquor herself. She is reported to have made $700,000 in one ten-month period. In 1928, when she was put on trial for violating Prohibition laws, her successful defense made national headlines.

In 1931 she tried to take her show, "Texas Guinan and Her Gang" to Paris, but by then her reputation was too risqué for the French; she and her show were deported. "Texas" promptly proclaimed that her show was "Too Hot for Paris" and asserted, "Fifty million Frenchmen can be wrong." She then toured the U.S. in a bus, proclaiming the cavalcade "Whoopee on Wheels!"

In addition to "Hello, Sucker!" the Waco native also coined the epithet "big butter-and-egg man" to describe a high-roller and Broadway "angel." Playwright George S. Kaufman even wrote a play by that name in 1925.

"Texas" Guinan died in November 1933, shortly after having repented her past, some said. She turned evangelist. Betty Hutton portrayed her in a romanticized film in 1940.

UNIVERSITY
OF TEXAS PEDAGOGY

Circular No. 16, issued by the University of Texas in June 1893, was titled "Announcement of Courses for Teachers, School of Pedagogy." The courses were taught by such UT luminaries as Leslie Waggener, professor of rhetoric and of English literature; Robert L. Dabney, professor of mental and moral philosophy and of political science; George P. Garrison, professor of history; H. Y. Benedict (who later became president of the university), tutor in mathematics; and Lester Bugbee, fellow in history. Joseph Baldwin was professor of pedagogy. "Candidates for admission must not be less than sixteen and must pass an examination in English," the circular stated. "Graduates of approved high schools, of the Agricultural College [Texas A&M], and of the Sam Houston Normal School . . . are admitted without examination."

It paid to finish high school: "Each year, the member of the graduating class in each affiliated high school who stands highest will be presented with a scholarship in the University . . . exempt from all University fees."

Undergraduate courses in pedagogy included:

Year 1: *Elementary Pedagogy:* Lectures and Baldwin's Art of School Management, Baldwin's Psychology Applied to the Art of Teaching, and Practice Teaching.

Year 2: *Advanced Pedagogy:* History of Education, Lectures and Pedagogical Library, Science of Education, Art of Teaching and School Supervision.

Year 3: *Professional Pedagogy:* School Systems, Methods of Governing and Teaching, and Current Educational Movements.

A final paragraph by Professor Baldwin exhorts: "Teaching as a profession now compares favorably with the other learned professions. Worthy teachers are held in high esteem and positions are becoming more and more permanent. Teachers' salaries have more than doubled in a single generation. Above all, modern teaching tends to develop grand men and women. There is no nobler or more inspiring work than teaching. Texas needs for her teachers thousands of her most gifted youths with the highest culture and the best professional education."

Women were assured that they were wanted in UT's recently created (August 25, 1891) Department of Pedagogy. The announcement circular of June 1893 noted that a matriculation fee of $30 was required, but board, with furnished rooms, "can be obtained at from $13 to $20 a month." Mrs. H. M. Kirby "assists lady students in finding good homes." The circular adds:

> The statute under which the University was organized states that "it shall be open to all persons in the State who may wish to avail themselves of its advantages, and to male and female on equal terms." Young women can enter this University with the full assurance that they will receive the benefits of its instruction on equal terms with young men. The Regents, in the appointment of Mrs. Kirby as Lady Assistant, have given assurance that young women will have all reasonable care in health and sickness. Mrs. Kirby is a lady of culture and refinement, and she has proven herself a devoted friend and companion of the young lady students.
>
> Gifted women seeking to prepare themselves for important positions are welcomed to the School of Pedagogy.

As with men, "The student . . . must be sufficiently mature to enter the School of Philosophy and take [a] course in Psychology."

Ten years later, according to the June 1903 University Summer Normal bulletin, we find several women teachers: Maud Margaret Shipe was tutor in the science and art of education; Roberta Lavender, instructor in Latin and Greek; and Alice Philena Hubbard, tutor in Spanish. Seventy-one of the 120 students enrolled are women. Railroads offer reduced rates to Austin, board and room remain the same as in 1893, and University Hall "will be open to both men and women. Men and women will occupy separate floors. A lady manager will reside in the Hall to look after the comfort of the guests."

Superintendent R. B. Cousins of Mexia comments: "I commend the authorities for opening University Hall to students of both sexes. I desire to bear testimony to the convenience and comfort of this delightful place."

THE GENTLE ART
OF DUELING

Although dueling was strictly forbidden in the Army of the Republic of Texas, Commander-in-Chief Albert Sidney Johnston set a rather bad example when, "as a public duty," he accepted the challenge of hot-headed but popular Gen. Felix Huston. Huston was enraged when Johnston was appointed senior general over him. The duel was fought on February 5, 1837, and Johnston, the future Confederate general, fell with a ball through his hip, lingering for days on the lip of death. The fragmented Texas army became united in hoping for his recovery, so, as Texas historian William Ransom Hogan wrote, "Perhaps the outcome was the best possible under the circumstances."

But too many duels were pushed upon nonaggressive men by bullies and professional killers as part of an assumed "code of honor." Some Texans scorned duels. President Sam Houston once returned a challenge with, "This is number twenty-four. The angry gentleman must wait his turn." When former President David G. Burnet challenged old Sam, Houston dismissed it with the remark that he "never fought downhill and never will." Nearsighted W. T. Jack once scuttled a challenge by proposing shotguns across a table as terms. Thanks mainly to Houston newspaper editor Dr. Francis Moore, Jr., a stringent antidueling law was passed by the Texas Congress in 1840. Until January 1, 1939, all state officials were required to take an oath that they had never taken part in a duel.

Knife-fights between eager opponents were another matter. Around 1842, Henry Strickland, "the Bully of the Tenaha," dueled Jim Forsyth via Bowie knife. Eph Daggett (later of Fort Worth) wrote: "Forsyth struck Strickland's right hand a little above the knuckle, cleaned all the flesh off four fingers clear to the bone. Strickland's knife fell, leaving him at Forsyth's mercy. He hacked [Strickland] on his arms, cleaving the flesh to the elbow with a downward lick, calling it 'trimming his marble.' Strickland turned and ran, but Forsyth followed and cut his shoulder blade in two, then let him go, declaring he only wanted to cripple Henry 'in order to make a pious man out of a rogue, a sponger, a horse thief and a peace disturber.'"

LOCKHART'S
LOVELY LIBRARY

Lockhart, county seat of Caldwell County, has retained a number of interesting and beautiful old buildings and homes. The Caldwell County Courthouse is an outstanding example of late-nineteenth-century Texas governmental pomp, spoken of in Lockhart as "ugly enough to be beautiful."

The Emanuel Episcopal Church, built in 1855–56, is one of the last buildings built of "rammed earth," which was fashioned from caliche, gravel, and wet sand, rammed down by hand to form a sort of concrete.

The modern City Hall is on the site of Susanna Dickinson Hanning's home. She was in the Alamo, recall, with her baby and her first husband, Almaron Dickinson, who died there. Known as "The Messenger of the Alamo," she was released by Santa Anna so that she could carry news of the fall of the fort to Gen. Sam Houston. William Barrett Travis's slave, Joe, was released with her to accompany her and her baby.

But the pride of Lockhart is the Eugene Clark Library. It is reported to be the oldest continuously used library in Texas. A two-story Classical Revival building, it uses a Greek cross plan. It originally had unusual auditorium-style seating and a small stage (where William Howard Taft once spoke), with books around the walls. One of the library's most engaging assets is the Irving Room, on the second balcony, where the Irving Club has met since 1900, using the same furniture—a priceless collection of quaint chairs and tables.

With its stained-glass windows, its dome, and its high steps, this lovely little library building is a downtown center. It was erected in 1899 with a $10,000 bequest from Dr. Eugene Clark, a New Orleans native whose father had been killed in the Civil War, when Eugene was only three. As the father lay dying, he requested his friend E. H. Purcell to take care of the son and wife. Three years later, Mrs. Clark, dying, entrusted the care of her young son to her dearest friend, Miss Helen Young.

The boy proved greatly satisfying to both Miss Young and Mr. Purcell. He graduated from Tulane Medical School with highest honors in May 1883 and moved to Lockhart, where he entered practice with a Dr. Lancaster, who soon abandoned his practice, leaving it to Dr. Clark, then aged twenty-one. After thirteen years in Lockhart, Dr. Clark moved to San Antonio, becoming an ear, nose, and throat specialist. He fell gravely ill and on his deathbed dictated a will to Mr. Purcell and Miss Young, specifying funds for the Lockhart library.

W. LEE O'DANIEL

Wilbert Lee "Pappy" O'Daniel, the nation's first "media" politician and one of the most successful in Texas history, was born in Ohio (1890), raised in Kansas, and didn't arrive in Texas until 1925, when he became sales manager, and later general manager, for Burrus Mill and Elevator Company of Fort Worth.

O'Daniel believed in advertising and decided that radio was the vehicle to sell his company's Lightcrust flour. In 1931, he hired a Fort Worth musical group, consisting of such now-famous musicians as Bob Wills, fiddle; Herman Arnspiger, guitar; and Milton Brown, vocalist. He first named the group "the Fort Worth Doughboys." This group then became "Lightcrust Doughboys," with O'Daniel as master of ceremonies for its daily statewide radio show. The Lightcrust Doughboys toured the Southwest in their own specially built bus, appearing at public gatherings for free, broadcasting from their bus, and generating huge crowds. O'Daniel also wrote songs for the group, composing several successful tunes in what then was called "country" or "hillbilly" style: "Put Me in Your Pocket," "Sons of the Alamo," "Your Own Sweet Darling Wife," and a song that became a sort of state anthem, "Beautiful, Beautiful Texas."

O'Daniel was no rube, although he played in the direction of the folksy philosopher in his radio talks and public appearances. Actually he was a very shrewd businessman. In 1935 he began his own company, Hillbilly Flour, with a new radio band, the Hillbilly Boys, which included Leon Huff and "Take It Away, Leon" McAuliffe. A line from the Hillbilly Boys' theme song, "Please pass the biscuits, Pappy!" gave O'Daniel his nickname. (The theme song itself was an adaptation of the popular hillbilly song, "I Like Mountain Music.")

By 1938, O'Daniel was the most popular radio figure in Texas, reciting poems and tales of Texas and American heroes. That spring, after his talks had become more populist in their tone, he began to get requests that he run for governor. On the advice of Reuben Williams, a young attorney, O'Daniel asked his radio audience what he should do. Within a few days he had received more than 54,000 positive replies. He announced his hat was in the ring, his platform "the Bible and the Ten Commandments." With his band playing his composition, "Got that

Million Dollar Smile," he swept the Democratic primary, despite the opposition of every newspaper in Texas and, among his twelve opponents in the race, such pros as Attorney General Bill McCraw, Railroad Commissioner Ernest O. Thompson, and third-time candidate Tom Hunter. Although he couldn't vote for himself—he hadn't paid his poll tax—O'Daniel won without a runoff.

His administration was immensely popular with the people—for one thing, he wanted to kill the poll tax—but was much less effective with the legislature. He continued his populist stance, such as inviting the whole state of Texas to his daughter Mollie's wedding. It had to be held in Memorial Stadium at the University of Texas, with free barbecue for the guests. In 1940 he won a second term, using his own prophetic theme, "There Ain't Gonna Be No Runoff (We don't have them anymore; we did away with runoffs when O'Daniel ran before)." Most of his foes in the legislature suffered defeat. In 1941, he defeated twenty-nine candidates, including Martin Dies and Congressmen Lyndon B. Johnson (the only defeat at the ballot box LBJ ever suffered), in a special election for U.S. senator. And in 1942 he defeated two former governors for the full senatorial term, all without a runoff.

But the U.S. Senate's clubby atmosphere broke the heart of O'Daniel, a true populist, and in 1948 he declined to run again. As he literally was cleaning out his desk, his last act as a senator was to appoint a young Texarkana man to the U.S. Naval Academy. That young man was H. Ross Perot. O'Daniel returned to Texas and operated a Fort Worth insurance company. Politics was in his blood, and he ran for governor in 1956 and 1958. But the O'Daniel magic was gone. He finished third in both races. He died in Dallas in 1969.

The
State
of West
Texas

WEST TEXAS

West Texas is the last frontier of the Lone Star State—still full of unsettled, late-settled, and sparsely settled regions. It really is too big to be evaluated as a whole, yet history and tradition have made it into a single province. West Texas has huge segments that are so different from each other that it seems impossible for there to be any kinship between them.

Central West Texas, which is the area most people picture as archetypal West Texas, reaches from the Brazos River to the Pecos, and from the upper Edwards Plateau, to the south, to the three-hundred-mile-long Caprock to the north.

Far West Texas, officially referred to as the Trans-Pecos, or "West of the Pecos [river]," is totally unlike nearby central West Texas, and puts the lie to the concept that all West Texas is flat and deserty. There are numerous mountains west of the Pecos that are higher than anything east of the Mississippi.

Far north of central West Texas lies the Panhandle. It was the final region of Texas to succumb to the invasion of white civilization. It is the former domain of the buffalo and, after the eighteenth century, Comanche horsemen. This tall rectangle of level territory is thrust amidst New Mexico and Oklahoma, and while it is the great wheat and grain producer of the southwest, the Panhandle is also the one part of Texas that annually has highway closures due to snow.

At the southern edge of the Panhandle and overlapping it for several hundred square miles, lies the High Plains region. The High Plains rise abruptly above the Caprock escarpment in a rich agricultural tableland extending northward to blend with the Panhandle. Like the Panhandle, much of the High Plains was not developed until the twentieth century. The Panhandle and the High Plains share the terrible Llano Estacado (Staked Plains), which once stimulated myths and legends of both fabulous wealth and dry, tortured death. Now it is a center for wheat, cotton culture, and cattle ranching, hundreds of thousands of acres being irrigated with underground rain from the Ogalala Aquifer.

Far West Texas is as large as many eastern states and has numerous subdivisions within it: the Big Bend, with the Big Bend National Park; the Davis Mountains; the Guadalupe Mountains and Guadalupe National Park (Guadalupe Peak, at 8,761 feet, is the highest point in Texas); the Chisos Mountains; the separate world of the upper Rio Grande; and the area around the city of El Paso. While historically the sixteenth- and seventeenth-century gateway to the Southwest, Far West Texas still contains thousands of square miles of virtually unknown mountains, canyons, and deserts.

Guadalupe National Park is more like Colorado than Texas, and the Davis Mountains, with their mile-high configuration, give cool summers unknown in most of Texas. At famous McDonald Observatory, near Fort Davis atop 6,800-foot Mount Locke, a July midnight can bring out visitors' coats and sweaters. Legend says that the Chisos Mountains, containing Big Bend National Park, are ghost mountains that disappear and reappear magically—a legend based on the fact that the light and clouds often obscure or mask the peaks.

The central prairie area, with its rolling and broken terrain, is a land that stretches under a long corridor of clouds, enticing artists to try and capture some of the allure, or dismay, of the land. Central West Texas is the Big Country, as the region around Abilene likes to call itself, following a famous movie of that name. It might justifiably call itself the Big Ranch Country, especially as you move northward. Storied for cattle, this central section also is the major sheep and goat producer of the nation.

Many West Texas cities began as railroad towns, as the old Texas & Pacific built westward from Fort Worth: Abilene, Big Spring, Odessa, Midland, and Pecos once were mere mileposts along that railroad. Other West Texas cities grew from historic associations: San Angelo, which began around the frontier post of Fort Concho; or Albany, which inherited the remains of the town of Fort Griffin (The Flat) when that government outpost was closed. The city of Fort Stockton contains the remains of the fort, established before the Civil War; and a newly renovated section of Fort Davis is within the community boundaries of the town of Fort Davis. Snyder, in Scurry County—where the last real Texas oil boom took place in 1949–50—started life as a dugout store supplying goods to the buffalo hunters. And West Texas is full of oil towns. Some, like Ranger, Wink, and Andrews, are much diminished from their heyday. Others, like Best and Texon, have disappeared.

Some major West Texas cities are "West Texas" more by geography than by choice. El Paso, despite the popular ballad concerning "the West Texas town of El Paso" and the city's location at the farthest western point of the state, does not always wish to be included in that cultural description, "West Texas." Amarillo, in the center of the Panhandle, is closer to four other state capitals than it is to Austin. Lubbock, on the other hand, argues fiercely when it is left out of a West Texas inventory, or when, despite being nicknamed "Hub of the Plains," it is lumped in with the Panhandle. Wichita Falls (which rebuilt its falls not long back) historically is a part of West Texas, but, as has been pointed out, it can be included in North Texas.

West Texas has minerals other than oil. It mines talc, cinnabar (sometimes), and gypsum—and once dug tons and tons of coal. Thurber, the major coal mining city in Texas (today it's the best-known ghost town), was an international community with miners from Hungary, Italy, and Central European regions. West Texas, in recent years, has gained two new "industries." Around Lubbock are found some of the most successful Texas wineries; and the length and breadth of West Texas now supports new state prisons, more than two dozen of them, giving new life to some of the victims of agricultural change.

All those separate parts of West Texas, being as they are so vast and so apart from the larger cities, have a number of individualistic small towns: Albany, with an astonishing aura of big-city advantages; Alpine, high and modern, with Sul Ross State University a collegiate world operating almost separately from the other state universities (Sul Ross teaches ranching, for one thing, and has an intercollegiate rodeo team). And many other towns unlike any others: Fort Stockton, Marathon, Marfa, and the cities below El Paso: San Elizario, Socorro, Ysleta.

El Paso, living on Mountain time, is the most unusual of the state's larger cities, being the only Texas city with true mountains within its city limits. With its Mexican counterpart, Ciudad Juárez, across the Rio Grande, it forms the largest population group on the U.S. Mexican border.

West Texas is the home of the cowboy, who is still in place on the ranches despite predictions of his demise since the opening of the twentieth century. The cowboy's working range starts in that central West Texas heartland that stretches from the Brazos River on the east to the Pecos River on the west, and northward high up in the Panhandle. While the pickup and the motor car tread the roads, the man on horseback still is needed to go into the breaks and thickets and roust out the stubborn steers.

The wide open spaces of West Texas tend to lead to a wide open society, to speed of decision and movement. This land raises great resentment in some people, and fears of dwelling under so much sky and in so much space—fears that urge flight. But in others this starkness and openness becomes the kind of beauty that cannot be abandoned, can never be erased. On this land was established the righteous dogma of individualism, leading to that highest of West Texas accolades: "He's his own damn boss!" (Or, increasingly, "She's her own boss!") A lot of that attitude prevails in West Texas.

But the fame of West Texas is not for its frontier history, its oil industry, or even its cowboys and ranches. Its fame is for its people. When you tell a listener from another "state" that someone, be it he or she, "is a West Texan," the listener seldom requires further identification. West Texans are reputed to be friendly and open-handed, glad to stop the pickup for someone in trouble. They have become gamblers when it comes to taking a chance; the cattle and oil businesses have taught them the necessity of that. West Texans are full of genuine hospitality and good humor. Terrible drivers! Above all, they are famous for not taking themselves, or life, too seriously.

While all this is generally true, the West Texan is not always viewed sympathetically. As one West Texas book puts it, "People who do not like West Texas frequently do not like West Texans, for the land is too strong in them . . . and it is an excessive land."

FORT PHANTOM HILL

Despite its ghostly sounding name, Fort Phantom Hill was not the home of specters or other disembodied spirits, although in the many years since its founding in 1851, all sorts of myths have sprung up about how the name was given, including stories by Emma Johnson Elkins, a nineteenth-century writer who was born on the post. One such is that, the first night United States soldiers were camped there, they espied four tall, blanketed Indians observing them, then dissolving into thin air. The hill itself supposedly was sacred to the Indians, the site variously said to be an Indian burial ground or the scene of "ghost" dances. The phantom idea has inspired several fictional plots, too.

Unfortunately for myths and stories, the Phantom Hill name came from an ordinary phenomenon. When approached from certain directions there seems to be quite a rise, but when the spot is reached, it seems flat—in other words, it is a phantom hill. It had been called that well before the fort was constructed, beginning in November 19, 1851. The site probably was first noted by Capt. Randolph Marcy, mapping a trail for California-bound forty-niners, from Fort Smith, Arkansas, to Dona Ana, N.M. Today his trail from the east, or the trail of the Butterfield Overland Mail, which in 1858–61 had a station at the fort, cannot be driven because farmlands there are plowed and fenced.

Other stories about the old fort claim that Robert E. Lee was its commander, or that he had a child buried there; but, in the first place, he was at Camp Cooper, several miles downstream on the Clear Fork River. He visited the fort after it was abandoned, but neither his wife nor any young Lee children came to Texas.

The post was established by Lt. Col. J. J. Abercrombie with 271 men from Fort Washita. It never was officially named "Fort Phantom Hill" but was titled, simply, "Post on the Clear Fork of the Brazos." Colonel Abercrombie was generous in bestowing his name on places (a Minnesota fort was named in his honor), but he only tried to name the range of hills and a prominent peak in what is now the Callahan Divide, a few miles southwest of the fort.

The powder magazine (still standing) was all rock and was once sheathed inside in copper to protect against sparks. Many of the numerous buildings had a stone chimney, most still standing, although the buildings themselves were little more than huts of *jacal* or log. The Butterfield station was in the rock guardroom, also standing. The grounds of the fort are privately owned but are open to visitors, with signs designating certain locations.

There exists a packet of letters from Lt. Clinton Lear to his new wife, who was back at an Oklahoma post. They were written from the first day (or night) on the fort site. Enthusiastic the first day, Lear within a week is complaining about the site and the quality of the water ("gyp"); "we can find [nothing] to indicate this [country] was ever intended for man to inhabit." Ironically, a long-time major water supply for Abilene, now a city of more than 110,000 residents, is Fort Phantom Hill Lake, located just a few miles south of the old fort site.

The fort didn't last long. It was abandoned on April 6, 1854, and 1st Lt. Newton C. Givens, the last commander (who has his own place in Texas history), is said to have sent back a slave and a soldier to burn the place so that no one else would ever have to endure serving there.

ROBERT E. LEE IN TEXAS

In the early 1850s, the U.S. Army established a string of forts across western Texas to protect settlers from the Comanche Indians, the finest horseback raiders in American history. With typical bureaucratic planning, these outposts initially were garrisoned by foot soldiers. But in 1855 the army came to its senses and organized two cavalry regiments. In 1856, Lt. Col. Robert E. Lee was sent to Texas to command two squadrons of the 2nd Cavalry at the raw and isolated Camp Cooper, on the Clear Fork of the Brazos in present-day Throckmorton County. Lee had been in San Antonio in 1846 during the U.S.-Mexican War, but in recent years he had been superintendent of West Point. He didn't like his new Texas duty, writing to Mary, his wife, "My military career is at a dead end."

But the months Lee spent at Camp Cooper helped to create the Civil War military genius. Although he had been a hero in the Mexican War, this was his first independent field command. In Texas he learned to decide and to act alone. His narrow aristocratic background dropped away, and his fabled human understanding emerged. From a man who had seen death many times—often at his own command—Lee's experience at Camp Cooper is revealing. He wrote to Mary, "For the first time in my life I read the beautiful funeral service of our church [Episcopal] over a grave." This happened twice within two weeks for young sons of military personnel, one of whom, he wrote, "I was admiring . . . [only] the day before he died."

Lee left Camp Cooper in mid-1857, and by then it was "my Texas home." After a period in Virginia, where he was put in charge of the Marine platoon that captured John Brown at Harper's Ferry, Lee returned to Texas and unsuccessfully pursued Juan Cortina, the legendary Texas-Mexican border bandit. Lee was at Fort Mason in February 1861 when ordered back to Washington. Texas already was a de facto member of the Confederacy, and a hot-headed San Antonio group almost lynched Lee at his hotel when he refused to say where his sympathies lay. (In January he had written, "Secession is nothing but Revolution. I wish no other flag than the Star Spangled Banner.") He left Texas on February 22, 1861, and returned to his home at Arlington, Virginia. President Abraham Lincoln offered him a top federal command in April, but he accepted a Virginia commission instead—and the rest is history.

Some have expressed doubt that Robert E. Lee's Texas stay exercised much influence over his subsequent Civil War career. Many of his biographers, including Douglas Southall Freeman, give scant space to his Texas experiences. But a study of his letters to Mary and his own response to the frontier seems to support its importance in creating the Robert E. Lee of history. Carl Coke Rister's *Robert E. Lee in Texas* (1946) gives a detailed account of those years.

THE GOLD RUSH

By 1850, California gold fever had swept the nation, and on March 12, 1850, a group of Dallas County residents from near Lancaster, led by Norvell Winniford and his new wife, Malinda Goar, left on a trek after riches. Among the goldseekers were Norvell's brothers David and nineteen-year-old W. J., Dan Clepper, Arch Lavender, John Milsap, Colonel Moss, and a man simply called "Pony." A man named Baker, crippled by rheumatism, went for his health, not gold. Most of the prospectors were young, inexperienced—not always wise.

Leaving Dallas County, their wagon train crossed the Brazos at Marlin and halted at Austin, where more Dallas prospectors caught up, including Pad Smith, Burt Crutchfield, Jess Tarky, Pat Hinkle, Jess Starkey, Will Morgan, and Ash Slayback. At San Antonio the full caravan of forty wagons assembled and headed for El Paso. Fifty-nine years later, W. J. Winniford wrote about the adventure in the old *Lancaster Herald*.

Now did you ever notice that in a big crowd traveling together there is sure to be some smart alick [*sic*]? Well, we had two of them and they came near getting us in trouble more than once. After traveling about 20 miles up the Pecos [River] we saw our first Indians. One of them swam the river and came to us, and by signs gave us to understand they had been following and watching us for several days, and by making signs with his hands and arm like someone playing the fiddle, for we played every night, asked permission to join us in our sport for they loved music. Ash Slayback, one of the smart alicks in question, jerked out his six-shooter and wanted to shoot him down without ceremony . . . and when we would not let him he shot at the bunch across the river. We threatened him that if any harm came of it, rather than be murdered ourselves we would turn him over to the Indians. You bet he was scared, but no harm came of it. We never saw the Indians again.

After leaving El Paso, an unbelievably stupid "joke" caused real tragedy. Winniford noted:

After putting out our pickets [guards], we were soon sound asleep, only to be awakened by the startling cry, "Indians! Indians!" Most of our men began running from place to place in the dark crying, "Where? Where?" Now Col.

Moss and me went to the north picket and found Jack Miller (although we didn't recognize him) lying in the high grass. He was a dark complected young man with long black hair and looked much like an Indian. He had a long blanket wrapped around him, evidently aiming to play a prank by making us think he was an Indian. When Col. Moss and I reached him, the Colonel demanded his name and to carry the joke further Jack only grunted as an Indian, and the Colonel repeated the question and was answered in the same way. Alas! poor Jack. Why didn't you tell your name? The next moment a musket ball pierced his heart. The crowd gathered in excitement and someone shouted, "Jack! come here, we have killed an Indian." But imagine our sorrow when it was said, "That's Jack Miller you have killed."

(W. J., in his memoirs, was sympathetic to the Indians, remarking, "Did it ever occur to you that the whites were the meaniest [*sic*] of the two?")

The Texas party reached the village of San Diego, California, on October 11, 1850, utterly broke, and after working to raise food money, arrived at the Calaveras River gold country on April 1, 1851. After fourteen months in the gold fields, Norvell and W. J., with four thousand dollars in gold between them, shipped from San Francisco to Panama, then to New Orleans via Cuba, and by flatboat to Shreveport and then on to Dallas County, arriving home on August 31, 1852. Among the several Texans who died on the trip were Norvell's wife Malinda and their premature baby and Norvell's brother David. W. J.'s recollection was that brother David died of a fever on Christmas Day, 1850. "He simply went to sleep."

But what Norvell and W. J. apparently never knew about their brother was that he lived on for years in Oregon. In 1952, a David Winniford IV appeared at the old Winniford homestead at Lancaster and related that his great-grandfather David had been left for dead on the California desert but a wagon train had come along to find the dying man "with a clammy fever" and nursed him back to health. David had never written to let his Texas family know he was alive—possibly because he felt he had been deserted, although W. J. is quite specific about the "facts" of David's death.

Norvell Winniford married two more times. During the Civil War, he was associated as a gun runner with William Marsh Rice of Houston, who moved his business to Matamoros. (Rice, in his will, left the money that later created Rice Institute, now Rice University.) Norvell Winniford was appointed "Reconstruction" sheriff of Dallas County in 1867. He died in 1885. The family stories came from Ella Winniford Taylor, of Texarkana, Texas.

CYNTHIA ANN'S
BROTHER JOHN

Cynthia Ann Parker is the best-known Indian captive in Texas annals, but few historians have taken note of her younger brother, John, abducted by the Comanches along with her. The two were taken on May 16, 1836, during a raid on Parker's Fort, Limestone County. Several members of the Parker family were killed; and a cousin, Mrs. Rachel Plummer, and her son James, also were taken captive. Cynthia Ann, aged nine at the time of her abduction, became the wife of Chief Peta Nacoma (Nocona) and mother of Quanah Parker, the last great Comanche war chief. She refused to return to the white world until retaken by rangers in 1860.

John, aged six when taken, quickly joined his captors. Some historians have written that he never was recovered, but others say his uncle, James W. Parker (Rachel Plummer's father), ransomed both him and his cousin Rachel at Fort Gibson, Indian Territory, early in 1843. Later John was induced by his mother to return to the Comanches and try to bring back Cynthia Ann. In 1852, U.S. Army Capt. Randolph Marcy wrote, "On his [John's] arrival [in Comanche country], she refused to listen . . . saying that her husband, children, and all that she held most dear, were with the Indians and there she would remain." John stayed with the Comanches also.

While on a raiding party into Mexico, John Parker fell in love with a Mexican captive, Juanita, and when he came down with smallpox, on the desolate Llano Estacado, the tribe abandoned him but Juanita stayed with him and nursed him back to health. Disappointed in the tribe, they returned to Mexico and were married. John became a rancher there and never returned to the tribal life.

Although remaining thoroughly "Indianized," during the Civil War he served the Confederacy with a Mexican company—the existence of which is seldom recorded. However, he refused to leave Texas and serve in Louisiana. He returned to Chihuahua, "never to cross the Rio Bravo again," as one version has it. In 1884, several years after they had all "walked the white man's road," Quanah Parker and two other Comanche chiefs visited Quanah's Uncle John in Mexico. John Parker remained "Indian" in dress and habits and enjoyed a long life as a successful Mexican rancher, reportedly leaving many descendants at his death in 1915.

THE DOVE CREEK FIGHT

In stories of frontier Texas, one seldom hears of Texans being defeated by Indians, but in the Dove Creek fight of January 8, 1865, a few miles south of present-day San Angelo, that is what happened. A large frontier force was routed by Kickapoos, who were moving from Kansas to Mexico to join tribal kinsmen. Apparently they were attempting to stay as far from the white settlements as possible, but they didn't want to stray too far west into the Comanchería, because the Plains Indians were enemies.

A group of Texas frontier militia under Capt. S. S. Totten of Bosque County—a stern disciplinarian, "which made him unpopular with certain classes," one officer reported—first discovered the Indian movements into West Texas after a scout from Fort Phantom Hill reported finding evidence of a large group. Totten was supposed to combine his force with Confederate troops under Capt. Henry Fossett at Fort Chadburne, but Totten disregarded the order and went his separate way to trail the moving tribe. Eventually, but only on January 8, the two Texas groups united, the Indian encampment having finally been located.

No attempt was made to identify the tribe (the Kickapoos from Kansas were not Texan enemies). Fossett possibly overestimated the Indian fighting force at between 400 and 600. The combined command of Texans was about 480. Both Totten and Fossett were criticized bitterly for their inadequate planning. In the first place, neither attempted to ascertain if the Indians were peaceful. All Indians were bad Indians, by their frontier philosophy. The Kickapoos had, in fact, been given passes by U.S. Army officers in Kansas, explaining that the tribal members were trying to get to Mexico and were not on a raid. Given the temper of the times, however, the passes might not have helped them in Confederate territory.

One general later reported, "The two Texas commanders, without any council of war, without any distribution of orders, without any preparation . . . gave the command 'forward!'"

The results were disastrous for the Texans. The Indians not only were well entrenched but had better equipment (Enfield rifles) than most of the Texans and used ambush strategy well. Within minutes, the militia (for they were not Texas Rangers, as is sometimes believed) were routed, losing three officers, including Capt. N. M. Gillintine, the leader, and several more men. The militiamen did not return to the field of battle, and toward the end of the day's fighting, the Confederate retreat "became a wild panic like the herd of stampeded cattle." A cold rain turned into a heavy snowfall, and the Confederate troops and the militiamen spent a miserable night and day before retreating back to John Chisum's ranch, a few miles south. Texans lost twenty-two killed, including five officers, and nineteen wounded. Upon arriving at Eagle Pass, the Kickapoos told a reporter they lost twelve killed and eight wounded, with two of the wounded dying after arriving in Mexico.

One of the Texan commanders claimed there were Union "jayhawkers" among the Kickapoos, taking charge of Indian defenses, but this has been disproved. The Confederate troops were a frontier battalion. Few had seen battle. It was simply a Texan defeat.

BUFFALO HIDES

It has been asked why the great slaughter of buffalo for their hides waited so long to take place. Prior to about 1870, there were, literally, millions of the "shaggies" (as hunters called them) on the midwestern plains; then, almost of a sudden, they were gone, killed off in a decade by the professional hunters.

Why did this huge slaughter begin so late? The reason, like the reasons for so many American historical developments, was commercial. Untreated buffalo hides, unlike buffalo fur robes—skins tanned with the hair intact—were assigned little value because of tanning difficulties. The technology for making usable leather from the soft and spongy buffalo hides was a European secret. However, once the secret reached America, tanneries on both sides of the water were processing what had been unwanted skins into leather. By 1872, American dealers were actively seeking the hard, dried "flint" hides.

But the buffalo-skin trade already had reached significant proportions. According to T. Lindsay Baker and Billy Harrison's book *Adobe Walls,* "initially the buffalo skin trade was an almost exclusive preserve of the Indian," who killed the bison not only for his own needs but also to secure skins to trade with the white man. A commercial "book" of Indian-killed and Indian-prepared buffalo robes began in the 1830s. This trade had begun expanding twenty years before: as early as 1815, some 26,000 robes were being shipped down the Missouri River; a decade later, more than 184,000 were reaching New Orleans alone each year.

Buffalo robes purchased and bartered from the Indians sold strongly through the middle of the nineteenth century. The southwestern plains, of course, represented an important source of such Indian-prepared buffalo robes. One of the most significant trading companies in the region was Bent, Saint Vrain and Company, which operated the famous Bent's Fort on the Arkansas River in southeastern Colorado.

But even before the mid-nineteenth century, a few Americans were engaged in professional buffalo hunting, mostly for meat. Railroad construction crews in the West lived on buffalo meat, more or less, and such famous names as "Buffalo Bill" Cody (that's how he got his name), Matt and George Clarkson, and William Matthewson were hired to keep the railway food tables filled. However, it was not until the demand for flint hides grew that the unbelievable slaughter took place.

The great Texas herds, mainly in the Upper Panhandle, were among the last of the buffalo herds to be slaughtered. Several temporary "cities" were built to accommodate the hunters, such as Rath City and Reynolds. Snyder, which survived, was begun by "Pete" Snyder as a buffalo "store" with hide tents and dugouts. Some say that, based on the characters of some of the original inhabitants, Snyder was called "Robbers' Roost."

Brothers Josiah Wright Mooar and John Wesley Mooar grew up in Vermont but became the most famous buffalo hunters in Texas. In Kansas, in the winter of 1870–71, nineteen-year-old Wright Mooar hunted mainly for meat, shipping tongues and hams fresh, leaving the hide on, but that year tanners in the United States began converting buffalo hide into serviceable leather. In 1872, W. C. Lobenstein, a Leavenworth, Kansas, dealer—soon to be in Dallas—got an order from an English tannery for five hundred buffalo hides. He passed the order to Charles Rath, another famed member of the Texas hide industry, who offered part of the order to Wright Mooar. According to the late historian Wayne Gard, Wright, after filling his quota, shipped fifty-seven extra hides to brother John Wesley, then working in New York City.

"When the hides arrived in New York, they were hauled down Broadway in an open wagon and attracted much attention," Gard wrote. "One of the men who saw them was a Pennsylvania tanner . . . who followed the wagon to Pine Street . . . where he offered to buy [hides] at $3.50 each" for experimental use. John Wesley Mooar quickly accepted the offer, which was over three times as much as raw hides were bringing in the West, and when Pennsylvania tanners ordered two thousand more, John Wesley joined his brother in the business of buffalo hunting, which ended in Texas in 1879. Wright Mooar also was famous for killing the last white buffalo.

After their buffalo-hunting days were over, the Mooar brothers married and settled in West Texas—John Wesley in Colorado City, where he died in 1918; and Wright on a ranch near Snyder, where he lived until 1940. When I was a small boy, my family and I went with our next-door neighbors, the Moores, to visit friends in Snyder, and it turned out that Wright Mooar either had a house next to the Snyder friends or was visiting nearby. At any rate, I met him and, along with the two families, heard some of his buffalo-hunting stories and other frontier tales. He was a very erect gentleman at the time and, as his name was pronounced the same as our Abilene neighbors, the Moores, I thought he was kin to A. D., the Moore son who was my playmate. Wright Mooar became one of my boyhood historical idols, although it was several years before I realized what a historical figure he really was.

Although most of the claims for the size of buffalo herds were exaggerated (one historian quotes a pioneer who said he saw a herd that covered fifty square miles), there is no question that millions of the shaggy beasts roamed the prairies of Texas and the Midwest. Buffalo meat is offered today as an exotic and tasty dish, but in the days of the great hunts, hides were what counted. In the middle of the 1870s, jerked (sun-dried) buffalo hams sold for three cents a pound in Dallas, while hides brought from one to two dollars each. It was estimated (possibly also exaggerated) that there were fifteen hundred buffalo-hide hunters in Texas alone in 1877. Fort Griffin, the city adjacent to the army post, was said to have sent two hundred thousand hides to market that one season, although by then the Texas herds were nearly wiped out.

Much latter-day abuse has been piled upon Texans and other frontiersmen for the wholesale slaughter of the American bison. But even at the height of the hunting, there were many who protested the killings and the waste of the meat. Several state legislatures passed laws to stop the devastation—although, in almost every case, such laws came too late. The Texas Legislature was on the verge of adopting such protective laws when none other than Gen. Philip ("Little Phil") Sheridan, then head of the U.S. Army in Texas, addressed the Austin lawmakers. The buffalo hunters should receive medals for what they were doing, General Sheridan said. He declared that the hide hunters "will do more in the next year to settle the vexed Indian question than the entire Army has done in the last thirty years." He pointed out that the buffalo hunters "are destroying the Indians' commissary." As for the hunters, "send them powder and lead, not censure. Let them kill, skin, and sell until the buffaloes are exterminated. Then your prairies can be covered with cattle and the festive cowboy, who follows the hunter as a second forerunner of advanced civilization."

Although Little Phil had been a Union general despised by most Confederate veterans, his prediction concerning the slaughter of the buffalo and the answer to "the vexed Indian question" proved at least partially accurate. After the hide hunters had done their deadly work, huge cattle herds soon replaced the bison as the major economic factor of West Texas, although, even as late as 1890, tons of buffalo bones were shipped out at great profit to the region.

BEN FICKLIN

Despite having been infamous with the Union as "The Mystery Man of the Confederacy" during the Civil War, dashing Benjamin Franklin Ficklin, by 1867, became the biggest mail contractor in Texas. He operated his "lightning lines" under government contract from Fort Smith, Arkansas, to San Antonio to El Paso, and (with Frederick P. Sawyer) out of Dallas to Sherman, Plano, McKinney, and other points. Ficklin, prior to the Civil War, had started in the stage business in Alabama, then he had gone west and is credited with being the person who thought up the Pony Express. Although quite handsome and a favorite with young people, he never married.

Ben Ficklin was born in Virginia in 1827 and at age seventeen entered Virginia Military Institute, where Thomas J. (Stonewall) Jackson was an instructor. But Ben pulled so many pranks—such as painting Old Coley (the superintendent's horse) red and white to resemble a zebra—he was kicked out a few months later. After service in the Mexican War, Ben returned to VMI and, despite his career in that war, was denied admission. He refused to budge from the superintendent's doorstep until finally reinstated. Then, as a descendent later wrote, "all 'L' broke loose again." When he graduated in 1849, Cadet Ficklin thrust his bayonet through his diploma and marched out of the hall with it on high.

During the Civil War, he was a Confederate purchasing agent, passing and repassing through federal lines, once returning through New York from London just to tease friends. In 1869, he bought 640 acres of Texas land three miles above Fort Concho and built the Concho Mail Station on an island in the North Concho river. A settlement grew up which manager F. C. Taylor named Benficklin, and when Tom Green County was organized, Benficklin was voted county seat. An 1882 flood washed Benficklin away, with a loss of sixty-five lives, and the county seat went to San Angelo. Ficklin's death occurred in 1871 on a visit east, when, at a dinner in Georgetown, D.C., a large fishbone lodged in his throat. Guests laughed, but it was soon evident that this was not another prank. When a doctor later attempted to dislodge the bone by pushing it downward, an artery was cut, and Ficklin bled to death.

Franklin Jones, the colorful Marshall (Tex.) lawyer, was a VMI cadet (Class of '23) with fond memories of pranks he and other 'Keydets' played, mostly on next-door rival Washington and Lee University. Jones, in a letter to a fellow "Brother Rat," as the cadets called each other, suggested, "Ben Franklin Ficklin's antics made subsequent ones look tame; therefore, I think we should work to have a 'Ben Ficklin Memorial Day' declared at the Institute."

THE NEW BANK AT BROWNWOOD

In the 1870s, as West Texas was opening up to white settlement, there were no banks. Citizens of Brownwood, for example, had to travel to Fort Worth, Waco, or Austin—each a hundred miles or more distant—to do banking. Brooke Smith and Otto Steffens, local merchants, decided that Brownwood (and their business) needed a bank, so they ordered an 8,500-pound safe from the Diebold Company in Ohio and announced the opening of the Pecan Valley Bank. Meanwhile, they stretched chicken wire across one corner of their store, erected a ten-foot plank counter (with an opening for Smith, the teller), and began doing banking business out of a wooden box.

Business was vigorous from the start, but some of the best potential customers were waiting for the arrival of the safe, feeling a bank without a safe wasn't a real bank. Finally the giant safe reached Texas and word was received that it was in Round Rock, as near Brownwood as the rails reached at the time. Smith and Steffens contracted the largest freight wagon they could find, and the safe was hauled by ox teams to Brownwood. For days the safe had been the chief topic of conversation in town. When it finally reached the outskirts, it was met by most of Brownwood's populace, "who," in the words of historian John Henry Brown, "made the traditional welkin ring."

A procession, which included most of the village wits, several overly imbibed males, and the inevitable line of boys, followed the safe and, amid much hurrahing and amateur "bossing," helped the weary freighters wrestle the monster into place. However, as the town stood by to await Smith's opening of the safe, it was discovered that the combination had not been sent, and the safe couldn't be opened. Since there were no telephones or telegraph in Brownwood, word to Ohio asking for the combination had to be dispatched by rider to be sent via Fort Worth. Thus, for its first month, the Pecan Valley Bank kept deposits and continued business in a box atop the beautiful safe. Not one cent was feloniously extracted, Smith reported.

Both Brooke Smith and Otto Steffens became known across the state as bankers. Steffens eventually moved to Abilene and headed a major bank there, and Smith had a station on the Fredericksburg & Northern Railroad named for him: Bankersmith.

THE NAMING
OF ABILENE

Late in the fall of 1880, several prominent men of the area met at the headquarters of John N. Simpson's Hashknife Ranch on Cedar Creek in Taylor County. The group included Col. Claiborne Merchant of Callahan County; his twin brother, John B.; J. T. Berry, a merchant of Belle Plain (now a ghost town, but then the seat of Callahan County); H. C. Withers of Dallas, a land man with Texas & Pacific Railway; and S. L. Chalk, a surveyor. They met with Simpson to talk about starting a town.

Years later, S. L. Chalk (who became Taylor County surveyor and historian) recalled the meeting: "After a fine ranch dinner they began the discussion." The railroad was eager to develop towns along its projected line from Fort Worth to El Paso, the sale of town lots bringing more initial return than freight or passenger revenues. The T&P had chosen a nearby site between Catclaw and Cedar creeks in Taylor County. The railroad was planning to call it "Tebo Switch."

The Merchants, Simpson, and Berry owned the land around the proposed site, and an agreement was signed with the railroad that a town would be laid out at a cost of $1.50 per acre, with land for depot, sidings, and cattle pens given to the railroad. The rest of the plat was to be divided fifty-fifty between landowners and railroad. The ranchers didn't care for the name "Tebo Switch," having a grander vision in mind. So they were allowed to name the proposed city. Clabe Merchant suggested "Abilene," in honor of the Kansas cattle town at the end of the Chisholm Trail, and they all agreed. The name, with the final "e" pronounced, comes from the New Testament (Luke 3:1) and, appropriately enough, means a prairie area. The Texas & Pacific railroad immediately began advertising its "Future Great" city—which irritated editors of some towns already in place, that considered themselves already great. By the time the rails arrived in mid-January 1881, the *Dallas Herald* was terming Abilene "the largest tent city in Texas." The town lot auction was held on March 15, with a crowd of merchants, cowboys, ranchers, buffalo hunters, gamblers, and land speculators bidding. Berry himself bought the first two lots for $710. They were well located; the mercantile section of Abilene grew up around them. The first child believed born in the new town was named Abilene, but unfortunately, the little baby girl lived only a short while and is buried in the earliest Abilene graveyard.

Hashknife headquarters, where the group met, was located on the brow of a hill near what is now Abilene Christian University. For years a depression in the backyard of a private residence marked the spot where the original ranch dugout had been. Simpson became an important Dallas financial figure.

Within a short time from its founding, Abilene, Texas, had outdistanced Abilene, Kansas, in population and commercial importance, although it never was able to overtake President Eisenhower's hometown in historical, literary, film, and electronic mythology as the legendary "wicked city" at the end of the cattle drives.

CRAZY WATER

The Palo Pinto–Brazos area, in what is now Palo Pinto and Parker counties, remained subject to Indian and desperado depredations as late as 1877. At that time Judge J. W. Lynch built a pole cabin on a site that is now downtown Mineral Wells and brought a little "civilization" to the immediate region. When first settled, it was noted that the water wells had an unpleasant flavor, but gradually this unpleasant water gained the reputation of being laxative and healthful—a common enough aspect of early Texas mineral-bearing water. Sour Lake, near Beaumont, had been a mineral spa for several years. President Sam Houston had visited the resort for his aches and pains.

The mineral water became the most thriving activity in the town of Mineral Wells. According to local legend, the name "Crazy Water" came from the beneficial effect the local water had on a woman visitor, supposedly suffering from some mania. Her family was traveling to California seeking a curative spa. The woman drank from a local 1885 mineral well and was cured of her mania. The well she is supposed to have drunk from is marked today by a historical plaque on U.S. Highway 180 where it meets U.S. 281 in downtown Mineral Wells.

With shrewd advertising, Mineral Wells began phenomenal growth, becoming not just a center for curative waters but a resort for all kinds of activities. The town is located in the hills of Palo Pinto County, and there is a natural charm to the rugged country. The nearby Brazos River, itself full of legends ("Lovers' Leap," "Inspiration Point," and so on), flows through the very heart of the county. Often called "the Carlsbad of America," Mineral Wells eventually had four hundred mineral wells. By 1910, over 150,000 patrons annually used its many hotels and bathhouses. A street railway line was built to accommodate visitors. Statewide conventions were a monthly event—for women's groups as well as men's. Mineral Wells gained an early reputation as a "suffragette town" because of the meetings there boosting women's voting rights.

Nearly every year some major political party held its state convention in Mineral Wells. By the later 1920s, thanks to its curative fame, the city had developed trained paramedical assistants, hospitals and other medical facilities, and a set of hotels untouched for splendor by almost anything in Dallas or Fort Worth. Among the famed hotels was the Octagon House (an eight-sided wonder); the Crazy Water Hotel, still standing; the Dameron; and the Baker—the latter as fine a hotel as existed in Texas, with a famous "million-dollar lobby" and an entire top floor devoted to its "Crystal Ballroom."

In the late 1920s, "Crazy Water Crystals" began to be sold in stores across the nation. Band leader Jack Amlung conducted his orchestra in a daily radio program from the Crystal Ballroom, advertising "Crazy Water Crystals." With its theme song, "Dream Train," it became the most popular show in the state.

"Camp Dallas," for ROTC cadets, for years was located at Mineral Wells, always a favored site for Texas military gatherings. During World War II, the town was home of Camp Wolters, and in the Vietnam War it was a major U.S. helicopter training center.

The medicinal-bathing period ended shortly after World War II, and Mineral Wells began a slow decline. Today the magnificent Baker Hotel is shuttered (though still guarded), and only a private bathhouse now and then is available.

JUDGE ROY BEAN

The legend of Roy Bean, "Law West of the Pecos," is so deeply ingrained in Texas lore—and Texans—that separating the truth from Bean's own personally enhanced fiction is almost impossible. Yet, this Texas "hero" has had at least two films made of his career, the 1972 version starring Ava Gardner and Paul Newman. His saloon, the "Jersey Lily," in Langtry, Texas, has been made into a state park visited each year by thousands of people from all over the nation.

Judge Roy Bean stories are numerous. When a dead man was found with forty dollars and a pistol on him, Bean fined the corpse forty dollars for carrying a concealed weapon. He is said to have dismissed a murder charge against a man who shot a Chinese workman, because "I cain't find nothin' in the law against killin' a Chinaman." Once, when Bean married a couple without authority, he gave them a divorce some time later "to rectify my error." When trains arrived in Langtry, Bean made it a point to be on the porch of the Jersey Lily, being himself a big tourist attraction.

Roy Bean admitted being a worshipper of Lily Langtry, the beautiful British actress for whom he named his saloon. Movie scripts to the contrary notwithstanding, he never met her (he was dead by the time she visited Langtry). And, legend to the contrary notwithstanding, Southern Pacific Railroad officials say the town of Langtry was named for a railroad construction foreman, not glamorous Lily.

Roy's biggest success was staging the 1896 Fitzsimmons-Maher world heavyweight championship fight in a ring erected on a sandbar in the middle of the Rio Grande, after the Texas Rangers had forbidden the fight on Texas soil. (It originally had been scheduled for a Dallas ring, but the governor intervened negatively.)

Born Phantly Roy Bean in Kentucky, he, at age twenty-three, joined his brother Sam and wandered the west, the con men leaving each state or community in a hurry. However, another brother, Joshua (later assassinated), was an important citizen of San Diego, California. Roy drifted to San Antonio during the Civil War, and a section of that town was long called "Beanville"—in his memory, but not necessarily in his honor. A fact often overlooked is that Roy Bean was married there in 1866 and had four children.

At age fifty-seven, with a tent saloon, he followed the railroad to Langtry. His title was one honest thing about him; the Texas Rangers named him a justice of the peace in 1882. He died in 1903. (It is believed his name, Phantly Roy, also the name of his father, was derived from the popular name "Fauntleroy.")

LARRY CHITTENDEN, POET-RANCHMAN

At the time he was writing, few poets in Texas were better known and loved than William Lawrence (Larry) Chittenden. Although a native of New Jersey, the fascination of ranch life caused him in 1887, at age twenty-five, to buy a ranch near Anson, Texas, and become a rancher and cowboy. He received a common-school education in New Jersey but had shown no particular turn toward poetry until his ranch days. Then he began writing verses, calling his poems "the offsprings of solitude—born in idle hours on a Texas ranch."

His rhymes were published in several Texas newspapers and in 1893 were gathered into a small volume titled *Ranch Verses*. The vigor and freshness of his rollicking poetry attracted favorable press notices nationally, and the book soon became one of the most popular in America, going into seventeen editions.

Chittenden, with the success of his writing, left the ranch after thirteen years and moved first to the Bahamas and then to Christmas Cove, Maine, where he kept a sort of resort hotel for visitors—especially those from Texas. He insisted on calling himself "Poet-Ranchman of Texas" long after leaving the state. He died in New Jersey in 1934.

Today, Chittenden and his verses are virtually forgotten, except for one poem, "The Cowboys' Christmas Ball," which begins:

> 'Way out in Western Texas, where the Clear Fork's waters flow,
> Where the cattle are "a-browzin'," an' the Spanish ponies grow;
> . . .
> Where the cayotes come a-howlin' 'round the ranches after dark,
> And the mocking-birds are singin' to the lovely "medder lark";
> Where the 'possum and the badger, and rattlesnakes abound,
> And the monstrous stars are winkin' o'er a wilderness profound;
> . . .
> Where the antelope is grazin' and the lonely plovers call—
> It was there that I attended "The Cowboys' Christmas Ball."

MOLLIE ABERNATHY

Mollie D. Abernathy was one of the truly legendary ladies of Texas, a celebrated cattlewoman and Lubbock pioneer. In 1900, her first husband, rancher-attorney James William Jarrott, located a strip of vacant land lying between two railroad surveys and reaching from Lubbock County to the New Mexico boundary—one mile wide and one hundred miles long. After he successfully filed on this strip (with twenty-four other families), the animosity of owners of adjoining ranches, who had been using the land without realizing that it was vacant, was so strong that a hired killer assassinated Jarrott in 1902. (The crime was confessed to by a convicted Oklahoma killer thirty years later.)

Young widow Mollie, despite dangerous opposition, took over and prosperously operated her "strip" ranch, part of the original survey. Her strip was one section wide (one mile) and sixteen sections long (sixteen miles). She stocked it with registered cattle, remarking to friends that her husband had paid such a price for it that she wouldn't dishonor his memory with a second-class operation.

Born Mollie Wylie in Hood County in 1866, she grew up at Thorp's Spring, and when Add-Ran College opened there in 1873, she enrolled in the first class—at age seven. This was allowed by the college, as there were no other schools. She married Jim Jarrott in 1886. She spent her summers working on her family's West Texas ranches until she was capable, her father said, of "doing anything a rancher can do," which included shooting a rifle and riding a horse "a-straddle," both considered to be unladylike in other parts of Texas.

After a three-year stay in Arizona, she and her husband Jim Jarrott returned to Texas in 1890. They settled at Stephenville, where Jim (who had served in the Texas Legislature) became county attorney for Erath County. They became parents of four children.

After the murder of Jim Jarrott, Mollie went into real estate in the new town of Lubbock and in 1905 married Monroe G. Abernathy, a real estate promoter. The town of Abernathy, Texas, was named for him in 1909, after it had been moved from its original location at Bartonsite. The town of Monroe, later changed to New Deal, also was named for Mr. Abernathy.

Mollie Abernathy died in Lubbock in 1960 at age ninety-six, remaining active in business and Lubbock social affairs up to the time of her death.

SHORTEST RAILROAD

The Acme Tap Railroad, of Quanah, chartered January 7, 1899, with 1.510 miles of track, was the shortest railroad ever chartered by the State of Texas. Due to a curious error in a later Interstate Commerce Commission Valuation Docket, a comma replaced the period in the mileage and little Acme Tap was described as "a single track line, extending from Acme to Agatite, Texas, 1,510 miles." This caused a stir in rail circles when it seemed, for a moment, that a major railroad had been built without anyone's knowing it.

As S. G. Reed, the late, great Texas rail historian put it, "The building of this track and the chartering of this road came about in a rather unusual way. There had for several years prior to 1899 been two cement plaster plants at Agatite. One had a private side track. The other (Salina Cement Plaster Company) did not. The Fort Worth and Denver City Railroad was willing to build a siding for the 'orphan' plant but the proposed route lay over land belonging to the rival plant, which refused to sell or lease the necessary right of way."

So the Salina Company, in order to gain the right of land condemnation given railroads under Texas law, took out a charter for a railroad operating from its plant over to the "high iron" of the FW&DC (now the Santa Fe/Burlington Northern). The Salina Company built its rail line while officials of the rival company watched helplessly. Although the other company had been paid for the small portion of its land the Acme Tap used, the officials nevertheless were fuming. For many years, the Acme Tap actually operated as a separate railroad—the rival plant even joined in its use, shipping via the Acme Tap and participating in the fees other railroads had to pay the independent agency. Then, in January 1914, the little road was leased perpetually to the FW&DC.

The operation of the Salina plaster plant ceased in 1931, and authority to abandon the Acme Tap Railroad was granted in January 1938, ending the relatively long career of the road so short that even some of the most authoritative listings of Texas rail lines fail to mention its birth, life, and death.

POLO FEVER, 1904

An interesting new branch of the horse business in West Texas had developed by 1904. It was supplying northern and eastern polo clubs with Texas ponies. William Anson, of Coleman, writing in the *Texas Almanac* for that year, notes, "While no systematic attempt has been made to breed polo ponies, conditions of climate and pasturage, combined with peculiarities of breed, have tended to produce an appreciable number of these highly prized and fleet-footed accessories to the rich man's game. By far the largest number, especially of the higher class [of ponies], come from Texas."

Texas horsemen in years past had interested themselves greatly in running short-distance pony races, mostly for a quarter of a mile. Many of the early settlers came from districts in Tennessee and Missouri, where this form of racing had been popular for years. They brought descendants of the famous "Steel Dust," a Texas horse, and other quarter horses to their new homes. They naturally endeavored to perpetuate and improve the quarter-horse strain. For this purpose, when outside blood was necessary, they selected the best of the pony-built mares of the country. Thus, when the demand arose for polo ponies, the Texas breeders found that they unconsciously had been breeding an animal almost ideal for polo purposes.

Dealers visited various ranches during the fall months, buying a pony here and there. The writer noted:

> prices varying from $60 for doubtful or otherwise risky purchases to $300 or even $400 for what they call "cracker-jacks." A sufficient number being acquired they are [sent] to the dealer's training quarters where they are put through a long course of education, sometimes with daily work for six months, at the end of which time those that have stood the test satisfactorily are shipped to the principal polo centers of the East—New York, Philadelphia and Boston—where they sell for large prices, as high as $2,500 having been paid for a particularly brilliant individual. With the growth of the sport in all the large American cities this is destined to play an important part in the livestock business of the State.

Eventually a polo team of cowboys was organized in the Abilene area by the West Texas Utilities Company, and some of the greatest players in America developed from this beginning. Polo today continues to be big in Texas. One annual charity event, "Polo on the Prairie" near Albany, drawing players from all over North America, has contributed more than one million dollars to the M. D. Anderson Cancer Center in Houston.

PERSHING IN TEXAS

General of the Armies John J. ("Black Jack") Pershing, the commander of the American Expeditionary Force in Europe in World War I, experienced his greatest personal defeat, loss of virtually his entire family, while in Texas in 1915.

General Pershing was stationed in El Paso as head of Fort Bliss and in charge of the United States Army's watch on Pancho Villa, whose roving banditry in northern Mexico threatened the Texas and New Mexico borderlands. A dispatch in the *San Antonio Express* of August 28, 1915, tells about the tragedy:

> Warren Pershing, 5 year old son of Brigadier General John J. Pershing, was rescued early today from his burning home at the Presidio of San Francisco in which his mother and three sisters, Mary Margaret, Anne, and Helen, were suffocated and burned. His father, Gen. Pershing, commanding troops on the Mexican border, left El Paso today, and U.S. Senator Francis E. Warren, father of Mrs. Pershing, will come from Cheyenne, Wyoming.
>
> Little Warren Pershing, the only one left tonight of General Pershing's family, is being mothered by nurses at the Letermann General Hospital at the Presidio. He was taken there today when he was picked up unconscious on the floor of his bedroom by officers and men who crawled through the burning house searching for Mrs. Pershing and her children. Warren revived quickly. The others were dead when the rescuers reached them, suffocated, and their hands and feet burned. Warren was found by Will Johnson, the Pershings' aged Negro servant, who led a rescue party into the house. In a corner of the room most burned, the rescuers found Mrs. Pershing dead on the floor with her arms across one of the children who was on the bed. In another bed was another child; the third lay on the floor. The bodies of all were considerably burned.
>
> Mrs. Pershing was Frances Warren, daughter of Senator Warren, chairman of the powerful committee on Military Affairs during the Republican control of that body. In 1905, Miss Warren married John J. Pershing, who was then a captain of the 15th Cavalry. The next year, by congressional action, Captain Pershing was raised to the rank of Brigadier General.

General Pershing, who acquired the nickname "Black Jack" when he served with black cavalry soldiers during the 1890s, was an expert horseman. By the time he became commandant of Fort Bliss in 1914, he already had become an avid polo player. He discovered that a group of ranchers in the Midland area was playing the game, and he was a fairly regular player with them, bringing his ponies, handlers, and other officers who played the game to Midland via rail from El Paso. After the deaths of his wife and daughters, he is said to have turned to the game to help alleviate his sorrow. The incursions of Pancho Villa along the Mexican border, in 1916 and 1917, forced Pershing to give up participation in the Midland games. He was transferred to Fort Sam Houston in San Antonio later in 1917 and was almost immediately made commander-in-chief of the AEF when World War I began in April.

TEXAS' FIRST FIRE TRUCK

The City of Big Spring believes that it was the first town in Texas to purchase a self-propelled motorized fire truck. This was early in 1909, a year or more in advance of such cities as Dallas, Houston, San Antonio, and Fort Worth.

Three devastating fires had ravaged the downtown section of the West Texas city in 1907 and 1908, proving that the volunteer "push wagon" brigades were dangerously inadequate. In addition to establishing fire zones and outlawing wooden construction in those areas, on April 1, 1909, the Big Spring city council accepted the proposal of the Webb Motor Fire Apparatus Company, of Vincennes, Indiana, to build a self-propelled fire engine that could pump water from wells and cisterns and also spray chemicals. The cost was $6,000, half of which would be paid by Big Spring private citizens. A local driver was hired, at fifty dollars per month, to drive the truck and assist the volunteers. The first driver was fired when he allowed friends to take "No. 1" to the city park to play with it, according to council minutes.

The Vincennes plant where the Motor Fire Engine was built had been a stove works before being sold late in 1907 to A. C. Webb, a successful Saint Louis automobile and race-car builder. The Webb pumper of 1908 was reported to be the first combination hose and pumping apparatus on the market. Webb's machine was built on an Oldsmobile chassis, according to a truck industry history. The Webb fire engine factory lasted only four years, but the product did much better. Big Spring used No. 1 until 1925.

Big Spring researcher Mrs. Floyd Mays says that two other Texas cities contend they had fire engines earlier; Canadian, in the Panhandle, and Baird, near Abilene, claim such equipment purchases in 1906. However, the Canadian "truck" apparently was a mounted pump and tank, not a self-propelled vehicle. A search of city and county records at Baird failed to turn up any evidence of a motorized fire truck earlier than 1909, so the Big Spring claim to first ownership is felt to be historically solid.

B. C. Thompson of Arlington, commenting on the Baird claim, says:

> I lived at Baird from 1935 to 1954 and during my high school years I worked as sack-boy-stocker-janitor after school and on Saturdays at a grocery store on Main Street. The fire house was near, and anyone young enough to run the hundred yards or so to the trucks and old enough to drive was almost required to serve in case of a fire, since the department was all volunteer. During that period, Baird had a very old and big beast of a fire engine that was chain drive. My training consisted of two warnings, "Son, don't run this thang very fast; if that there chain flies off it'll go right through somebody's house," and, second warning, "When pulling out of the station, wait until you feel the arse end of the thang sink before tryin' to turn, otherwise you take off one side of the station."
>
> Eventually that beautiful old big truck was relegated to the back of the house, to be used only in dire emergencies. Do you think that truck could have been the one Baird claimed was older than 1909? If so, the Baird folks sure got a lot of service for their tax dollars.

THE HILTON
HOTEL CHAIN

The worldwide Hilton Hotel chain began as a small, two-story red brick hotel in Cisco, Texas, in 1919. Conrad Hilton, founder of the chain, arrived in the booming oil town to buy a bank, banking being his business in New Mexico. But the owner of the Cisco bank ultimately reneged on the price, and Hilton was forced to wait in town an extra day. This was during the famous Ranger (Texas) oil boom, and, although Cisco wasn't in the Ranger field, it, like other Eastland County towns, enjoyed the overflow from wealth created at nearby Ranger.

Unable to get a place to sleep, Hilton, the young New Mexico native, looked around and decided that the big money in that town was in the Mobley Hotel—which was sleeping guests in eight-hour shifts around the clock. As it turned out, the hotel owner was eager to be rid of the Mobley so he could get into the oil business. Although unfamiliar with the business, Hilton bought the little hotel and, in his autobiography, *Be My Guest,* wrote: "The Mobley, my first love, was a great lady. She taught us the way to promotion and pay, plus a lot about running hotels. She was indestructible, the ideal hotel to practice on."

Conrad's second hotel was the Melba, in Fort Worth. With the help of a young Dallas banker, R. L. Thornton (later to become famed as Dallas's "dydamic"—his word—"Uncle Bob" Thornton), Hilton bought a third hotel, the Waldorf in downtown Dallas. Then Hilton obtained the Terminal in Fort Worth, one of the city's finest, and expanded to Corsicana, where he leased the Beaton.

In July 1924, Conrad Hilton spaded the first dirt for a *Hilton* hotel, the Dallas Hilton, which opened in August 1925. The second Hilton hotel was built at Abilene, where a five-piece group led by a young accordion player named Lawrence Welk was the house band. Dixie Blanton, a professional "flagpole sitter," perched atop the new hotel in its first week, taking phone calls from all over Texas. Then, in rapid succession, Conrad Hilton added Hilton hotels in Waco, Marlin, Plainview, San Angelo, Lubbock, and El Paso.

In 1937, Hilton expanded what were billed as "The Mini-Max Hotels" outside Texas, to San Francisco. His first foreign hotel was the Palacio Hilton in Chihuahua, Mexico. Following World War II (and a stormy marriage to Zsa Zsa Gabor), Hilton opened hotels around the globe, the first American hotel chain to do so. In 1954, Hilton bought the Statler hotel chain, at the time the largest real estate transaction in history. In 1954 Hilton also took over the Shamrock, Houston's late glamour hotel, which Glenn McCarthy had opened five years before with lavish festivities that furnished the example for the film *Giant.* At his death in 1979, Conrad Hilton's chain, from its two-story, red-brick Cisco beginning, had grown to be one of the largest hotel systems in the world.

In the 1980s, thanks to the Hilton Corporation, the Mobley Hotel was made into a museum of Cisco history, the lobby and some rooms being restored and furnished in their boom-days condition. It is ironic, perhaps, that several of the larger, more magnificent Hilton hotels (such as the Shamrock) have been demolished; others, like the Statler-Hilton in downtown Dallas, have been sold; and many, such as the Hilton in Plainview, are boarded up. The Abilene Hilton now houses retirement apartments. But the Mobley, the old original, is open to the public.

ROBY & NORTHERN
RAILROAD

Texas has had many strange railroads, but none quite so startlingly out of place as the four-and-a-half-mile-long Roby & Northern Railroad in West Texas. Motorists traveling U.S. 80A (now U.S. 180) often were astonished to see a trolley car suddenly come flashing its way across the West Texas prairie.

The Roby & Northern ran from Roby, county seat of Fisher County, with a population of under nine hundred, to North Roby, a siding on the Waco-Rotan branch of the Katy Railroad, with no population at all. The little line was built originally as a steam road in 1915, using a tiny saddle-tank locomotive for motive power and a tin shack for its only station. Within six years, things were in such bad shape that mules were often called upon to pull the freight cars.

Citizens of Roby offered to help the West Texas Utilities Company, of Abilene, buy the railroad, and found an enthusiastic investor in Price Campbell, that firm's president. Campbell decided to make the R&N into the finest electric interurban railway in the United States, despite its remoteness. By the summer of 1923, a big labor force was relaying the tracks with heavier rail, constructing new culverts and bridges (the route had two bridges), and installing overhead wire for trolley propulsion. The sheet-metal station was replaced with an impressive new depot of brick, tile and concrete, topped by a flashing electric sign proclaiming, "The Best Short Line Railway in America."

The glory of the R&N equipment was No. 6, a 90,000-pound, sixty-foot-long trolley converted from a kerosene motor car originally used on the Nashville, Chattanooga & St. Louis railroad. This gleaming behemoth, the largest interurban car ever to run in Texas, had stained-glass inserts above its windows and carried mail, express, baggage, and passengers. It was powerful enough so that it could also pull a string of freight cars. Some five thousand people—more than the total population of Fisher County—attended the barbecue celebrating the new interurban's first run.

Things went so well that, in 1931, No. 7, a former Abilene streetcar rebuilt to handle mail, express, and passengers, was added to the roster. But trucks and highways, along with Roby's lack of growth, wrote the end of the R&N, and in July 1941, when the board of directors held its traditional annual luncheon meeting on the Clear Fork River bridge, midway of the line, they used No. 7 as a diner for the final time. The Roby & Northern made its last trip on December 31, 1941, with Price Campbell at the controller. Within weeks, the rails and big No. 6 had gone into a World War II scrap drive.

An interesting recent note: The town of Roby, much smaller than in 1941 and even more a victim of changing Texas economics, gained national attention early in 1997, when a group of twenty-two townspeople, most of them associated with Roby's last industry, the local cotton gin, won a $43 million jackpot in the Texas lottery.

CONAN'S CREATOR

In the 1920s and 1930s, my grandmother, Maude E. Cole, was Carnegie librarian in Abilene, my hometown. She was a writer herself and always kept a library table for the exclusive use of the small circle of writers who formed Abilene's literary corps. Writers and would-be writers from all around used to come to the library to ask her advice or merely to relate the problems of trying to be a writer during the Depression. One of those was a man from Cross Plains (a few miles southeast of Abilene) who occasionally did research in the Abilene library and once told my grandmother that he intended someday to do what he called "more serious work." I didn't meet him, but she would often mention interesting patrons at home, and she told me about him, because he was, as she put it, "so intense." I don't think his pulp work made any difference to her, because most of the Abilene writers were doing (or trying to do) pulp fiction, too.

Back when westerns, science fiction, and all pulps were the underside of American literature, the young man in Cross Plains was making a living—reportedly a good one—writing for these lowly organs. His name was Robert E. Howard, and while he may not have been the first sci-fi writer in Texas (one was reported as early as 1855), he nevertheless was, historically, the most important, for he created "Conan the Barbarian," made even more famous by Arnold Schwarzenegger decades later in movies and television. Howard wrote almost in secret. He lived at home and worked at home, and unless some resident of Cross Plains (pop. 1,500) saw his name in some magazine in the local drugstore, he didn't talk about his writing.

Born in Peaster, Weatherford County, in 1906, Robert Howard lived most of his life in Cross Plains with his father and mother, Dr. and Mrs. I. M. Howard.

Some science-fiction writers call his type of writing "Sword and Sorcery." Most of Howard's "Conan" stories are set in the Hyborian Age, some twelve thousand years before the Stone Age. Conan was not his only creation—there were Bran Mak Morn, Cormac MacArt, and King Kull, for instance. His writings are full of black magic, the occult, fantastic creatures. He once said he got his characters from dreams. But Texas sci-fi writer Chad Oliver says that Howard was "a far better writer than people give him credit for."

In 1936, Robert's mother, Hester, with a fatal disease, fell into a coma and could not recognize him. When told she could never recover, Robert went directly to the new Chevrolet he had paid cash for the season before (it was parked beside the modest frame house where they lived in Cross Plains), got in, and killed himself with a pistol shot. Today there are Robert Howard fan clubs, three bibliographies, an index to his characters, a biography, and a fan magazine, and there is no sign that his cult is dying off. And Schwarzenegger, with his "Conan" roles, launched his subsequently successful film career.

Author L. Sprague de Camp, Howard's principal biographer, in *Dark Valley Destiny,* wrote that Robert's suicide pistol was an automatic, "borrowed from his friend Tyson." De Camp, who was the grand old man of science-fiction, adds, "I suspect that Robert's father had hidden Robert's own pistol in fear of what actually happened."

Ironically, Dr. Howard, losing son and wife within two days, gave everything, including Robert's copyrights, to a friend who, in turn, left them to his daughter. After more than thirty dry years, the royalties poured in. Robert E. Howard would have become a wealthy, celebrated writer had it not been for an automatic pistol.

Index

Castle, Vernon, 102–103
Castro, Henri, 7
cattlemen: C. C. Slaughter, 87–89
Central Texas: boundaries of, 111; character of, 111–12; regions of, 111
chacon (goat meat), 121
Chalk, S. L., 148
Chambers, Thomas Jefferson, 24–25, 60
Chambers County, 25
Champ d'Asile, 18–19
charities: polo players and, 155
Cherokee Indians, 22, 24, 50
Chisos Mountains, 134
Chittenden, William Lawrence, 152
Cisco, 158
Ciudad Juárez (Mexico), 135
Civil War: cotton transport during, 71–72; John Bankhead Magruder in, 65; last actions of, 67, 117; Shelby Expedition and, 66–67; in South Texas, 44. *See also* Confederacy
Clark, Eugene, 127–28
Clarkson, George, 144
Clarkson, Matt, 144
Clayton, Will, 73
Clear Fork of the Brazos River, 6
Clear Fork of the Trinity River, 6
Clifton, John M., 21
Closner, John, 49
Clower, D. M., 89–90
Cockrell, Sarah, 96, 97
Cody, Samuel Franklin, 98–99
Cody, William Frederick (Buffalo Bill), 144
Coffee, Holland, 113
Coffee, Sophia, 113
Coke, Richard, 31, 117
Cole, Genoa, 57
Cole, Maude E., 161
Coles, John P., 73
College Hill, 115
colleges: McKenzie College, 82–83; Salado College, 114–15
Colorado City, 7, 35

Colorado River: Marble Falls dam and, 122; naming of, 17; steamboats and, 47
Comanche Indians: captives of, 141; Leonard Williams and, 22; raids of, 50–51; William Goyens and, 24
Commercial and Agricultural Bank, 54, 55
"Conan the Barbarian" (Howard), 161–62
Confederacy: anti-Southerners and, 86–87; burial of Confederate flag, 66; Dance percussion pistols and, 26–27; Dove Creek fight and, 142–43; Mexican colonies and, 66–67; symbolic burial of, 66. *See also* Civil War
Connally, John, 73
Cooley, Denton, 73
cooney, 15
Corpus Christi, San Diego and Rio Grande Narrow Gauge Railroad, 8
Cortina, Juan, 138
Cós, Perfecto, 55, 58–59
cotton: transport from Bagdad, Mexico, 71–72
cotton towns, 112
Council House fight, 50
counties: names of, oddities in, 6–7
Cousins, R. B., 125
Cowart, Robert E., 86
cowboys, 135
Cowboys and Cadillacs (Graham), 11
"Cowboys' Christmas Ball, The" (Chittenden), 152
"Cowtown" (Fort Worth), 78, 85
Cox, Joseph, 59, 60
Craig, Hiram G., 88–89
Crane, Royston C., 57–58
Crane, Royston C., Jr., 58
"Crazy Water," 149–50
Creekmore, Lefty, 9
Cross Plains, 161
Crystal Ballroom (Baker Hotel), 150
Cullen, Hugh Roy, 73
Cullinan, J. S., 72
Cummins, James, 73

Cunningham, E. H., 51
Custer, Elizabeth, 117
Custer, George Armstrong, 117

Dabney, Robert L., 124
Daggett, Eph, 126
Dallas: Alexander Cockrell and, 96–98;
    C. C. Slaughter and, 88; character of,
    78; early telephone lines in, 89–90;
    first automobile in, 94–95; Ford Motor
    Company and, 105–106; interurban
    electric railways and, 92; as "The
    Metroplex," 77; metropolitan area of,
    78; newspapers of, 35; professional
    athletics and, 78–79; relationship with
    Fort Worth, 85, 86; Sarah Cockrell and,
    97; terrorization of slaves in, 86–87; as
    "The Three Forks" area, 6
Dallas County jail, 92–93
Dallas Herald, 35
Dallas & Wichita Railway, 8
dams: at Marble Falls, 122
Dana, James D., 118
Dance brothers, 26–27
*Dance & Brothers, Texas Gunmakers of the
    Confederacy* (Wiggins), 27
Dance percussion pistols, 26–27
dancers: Vernon and Irene Castle, 102
Dane, Benjamin F., 116
Dark Valley Destiny (de Camp), 162
Davis, Edmund J., 117, 119
Davis, Jefferson, 6, 31–32
Davis Mountains, 134
de Camp, L. Sprague, 162
declarations of independence, 55–56
DeLeon, 18
Denison, Bonham and New Orleans Rail-
    way, 8
Destiny in Dallas (Seifert), 97
Devils River, 6
Díaz, Porfirio, 49
Dickinson, Almaron, 127
Dickinson, Susanna, 127

Dienst, Alex, 60
Dies, Martin, 129
Dimmitt, Philip, 55–56
dirigibles, 98
Dobie, J. Frank, xvi, 115
Donaldson, Nonna Smithwick, 60
Donna, 49
Dorris, George, 94
Douthit, Mamie, 57
Dove Creek fight, 142–43
dueling, 126

Eastland, Josephine, 122
Eastland, Wichita Falls & Gulf Railway, 8
East Line & Red River Railway, 8
East McAllen, 49
East Texas: boundaries of, 16; description
    of, 15–16; first European settlement in,
    17; proposed boundaries for, xvii
East Texas State University, 77
Edinburg, 49
Edison Company, 11
Ehrenberg, Herman, 57, 58
Elkins, Emma Johnson, 136
El Mejicano (newspaper), 35
El Paso, 134, 135
Emanuel Episcopal Church (Lockhart), 127
Erichson, Alex, 27
Erichson, Otto, 27
Escandón, José de, 69–70
Eugene Clark Library (Lockhart), 127–28
Evolution of a State (Smithwick), 113

Falcón, Miguel de la Garza, 69, 70
Fannin, James L., 58, 59
Fannin, James W., Jr., 56, 62
Fellowes, Georgina Kendall, 116
Ferguson, Miriam A., 115
Ficklin, Benjamin Franklin, 146–47
fights: at Council House, 50; at Dove
    Creek, 142–43. *See also* boxing; dueling;
    knife-fights
filling stations, early years of, 10

film industry, early years of, 11–12
firearms: Dance percussion pistols, 26–27
Fireman's Museum of Texas, 104
fire trucks, 104, 157–58
Fisher, Samuel Rhoads, 61–62
Fisher County, 62
Fitzhugh, E. H., 12
Fitzsimmons-Maher heavyweight boxing
    championship, 151
Five States of Texas, xv–xvi
Flanagan, James W., xvii
Fletcher, Mrs. Donna, 49
Flores, Juan, 85
Flowers and Fruits in the Wilderness
    (Morrell), 84
Foote, Henry S., xvii
Foote, Irene. *See* Castle, Irene
Ford, Francis, 12
Ford, Rip, 21, 63, 67
Ford Motor Company, 105–106
Fordyce, Sam, 49
Forsyth, Jim, 126
Fort Davis, 134
Fort Phantom Hill, 136–37
Fort Stockton, 134
Fort Worth: Canadian airfields at, 102; char-
    acter of, 78; "Cowtown" nickname, 78,
    85; "D/FW" designation for, 77; as mili-
    tary post, 79–80; newspapers of, 35; as
    "Panther City," 85–86; professional
    athletics and, 78; relationship with Dal-
    las, 77
Fort Yuma, 63
Fossett, Henry, 142
France: Champ d'Asile colony and, 18–19;
    Louisiana and, 16–17
Frantz, Joe, 30
freedmen: Harmony Settlement and, 28–29
freedom: in Texas history, xvi
Freeman, Douglas Southall, 138
Freeman, John, 84
Freeman, Nancy, 84
Fulton, George W., 46

Fulton (Arkansas), 81

Gaceta de Texas (newspaper), 35
Galveston, 90, 119
Galveston Island, 18, 19
Garay, Francisco, 57
Gard, Wayne, 144
Garrison, George P., 124
Garza Falcón, Miguel de la, 69, 70
gasoline, early quality of, 10
gas stations. *See* filling stations, early years of
"General Sherman" (locomotive), 52
geologists, 118
ghost towns, 60–61
Gillintine, N. M., 142
Givens, Newton C., 137
Glen Eden, 113
goat meat industry, 121
Gold Rush, the, 139–40
Goliad: declaration of independence, 55–
    56; massacre at, 56–57
Gonzales, Simón, 25–26
Goodnight, Charles, 85
Goyens, William, 23–24
Graham, Don, 11
Grand Duke (steamboat), 81
Grande, Rio. *See* Rio Grande
Grand Prairie, 104
Grant, George Washington, 28–29
Grant, Ulysses S., 65, 74
Grant's Colony, 28–29
Grant Springs, 28
"Grave of the Confederacy" incident, 66
Gray, Don I., 12
Great Britain: first powered flight in, 99;
    navy of, man-lifting kites and, 99
"Great Western, The." *See* Bowman, Sarah
Green, Edward Howland, 93–95, 96, 100
Green, Ely, 103
Green, Hetty, 93
Green, Thomas J., 60
Greene, Sarah, 35
Gringo Builders (Allhands), 49

captives of, 141; extermination of the buffalo and, 145–46. *See also individual tribes*
individualism, 135
Inglish, Betsy, 25
Ingramm, Ira, 56
Invincible (ship), 54, 62
Iron Brigade (Missouri), 66
Isabella (U.S. gunboat), 67

Jack, W. T., 126
Jackson, Claiborne Fox, 27
Jackson, Donald, 21
jails, 92–93
Jarrott, James William, 153
Jarvis, Tom, 53
Jasper News-Boy (newspaper), 35
Jefferson: *Jimplecute* newspaper and, 34–35; origins of refrigeration in, 46; steamboats and, 47
Jimplecute newspaper, 34–35
Johnson, Adam Ranking, 121–22
Johnson, Francis W., 59
Johnson, Lady Bird, 29–30
Johnson, Lyndon B., 30, 129
Johnson, Middleton Tate, 79
Johnson, William Weber, 31
Johnston, Albert Sidney, 126
Jones, Anson, 7, 116
Jones, Franklin, 147
Jonesborough, 81
Josher, The (newspaper), 35
journalists: George W. Kendall, 115–16
Jowell, Cynthia Ann, 88

Kansas City, Mexico and Orient Railway, 71
Karlshaven (Indianola), 60, 61
Karnack, 29–30
Katy Railroad, 11
Kaufman, George S., 124
Kell, Frank, 103
Kelley, Pat, 47
Kelly, George Addison, 30–31

Kelly, H. O., 31
Kelly Plow Company, 30–31
Kellyville, 30–31
Kemp, Joseph A., 103, 104
Kempner, Dan, 51–52
Kendall, George W., 115–16
Kendall County, 116
Kenedy, Mifflin, 71
Kerr, James, 64
Kiamatia Plantation, 81
Kickapoo Indians, 142–43
Kiest, E. J., 94
Kinetoscopes, 11
King, Richard, 46, 47
Kiowa Indians, 50, 51
kites: man-lifting, 99
Knapp, Seaman, 94
knife-fights, 126
Knox, John Armoy, 35
Kyle, W. J., 51

La Belle (ship), 44
labor, 73
La Feria, 49
Lafitte, Jean, 18, 19, 23, 71
Lafitte (steamboat), 54
Lallemand, Charles Francois Antione, 18–19
Lamar, Mirabeau, 50, 51
Lancaster, 90
land grants: to early Anglo settlers, 73
Langtry, Lily, 151
Lanham, S. W. T., 107
La Salle, Sieur de, 44
Latimer, J. W., 35
Lavender, Roberta, 125
Leadbelly. *See* Ledbetter, Huddie William
Lear, Clinton, 137
leather, buffalo, 143
Ledbetter, Huddie William, 15
Lee, Robert E., 7, 65; experiences in Texas, 137–38; Fort Phantom Hill and, 136–37
León, Alonso de, 6, 17–18

Leon River, 18
L'Heroine du Texas, 19
Liberty (ship), 54
libraries, 127–28
Lima Locomotive Works, 36, 37
Limestone County, 23
Lindsley, Philip, 87
Linnville, 50
Lisbon West of the Trinity (Anthony), 92
literature: Texas regionality and, xvi
Little Motor Kar Company, 10
Little River, 18
Littleton, Martin W., 106–107
Llano Estacado (Staked Plains), 133
Lobenstein, W. C., 144
Lockett, Zack, 30
Lockhart, 127–28
locomotives: "General Sherman," 52; 600-
    series, 36–37
Lonesome Dove Baptist Church, 84
Lonesome Dove (McMurtry), 84–85
Lone Star Motor Company, 10
Longley, Bill, 26
Longley, Mary Catherine, 33–34
Longview, 30
Lord, Walter, 59
Los Adaes, 16–17
Lott, Uriah, 49
Lotz, W. R., 35
Louisiana: colonial capital of Texas in,
    16–17
Loving, Oliver, 85
Lowe, Thaddeus Sobieski, 46
Lubbock, 134–35
Lucas, Anthony, 32
Lundy, Benjamin, 23
Lynch, J. W., 149

Magnetic Quill, The (newspaper), 35
Magruder, John Bankhead, 64, 65
Marble Falls, 121–22
Marcy, Randolph, 136, 141
Marlin, 120

Marshall, 21, 22, 27–28
Marshall & East Texas Railway, 8
Marshall University, 21
Martin, Lucy, 100
Matthewson, William, 144
Maximilian, Emperor, 64, 65, 66
Mays, Mrs. Floyd, 157
McAllen, 49
McAllen, John, 49
McCall, John B., 8–9
McCraw, Bill, 129
McCulloch, Alex, 46
McCulloch, Ben, 46
McDonald, William Madison, 94,
    99–100
McDonald Observatory, 134
McKenzie, John Witherspoon, 82
McKenzie College, 82–83
McKinney, Collin, 7
McKinney, Thomas Freeman, 54–55
McKinney and Williams Company, 54–55
McMurtry, Larry, 84–85
McNelly, L. H., 85
meat packing: early methods in, 68; goat
    meat canneries, 121; origins of refrigera-
    tion and, 46
Medina River, 17
Mèliés, Gaston, 11
Menard, Michel, 54
Mercedes, 49
Merchant, Claiborne, 148–49
"Messenger of the Alamo, The," 127
"Metroplex, The." *See* Dallas
Mexican War, 44; Sarah Bowman in, 63;
    troop performances during, 65; war
    correspondents in, 115–16
Mexico: Confederate colonies in, 66–67;
    cotton transport from Bagdad, 71–72;
    South Texas and, 44, 45
Milan, Ben, 58
millionaires, black, 23–24
mills: Mormons and, 113
mineral water, 119–20, 149–50

women: as teachers, 125; at University of
Texas, 125
Wood County: Martin Varner and, 25–26
Wootan Wells, 119–20
World War I: Royal Canadian Flying Corps
and, 102–103
Worth, William, 79, 115–16
Wright, Travis, 81
Wylie, Mollie. *See* Abernathy, Mollie D.

Ybarbo, Gil Antonio, 17
Yellowstone (steamboat), 19–21
Young, Helen, 127
Ysleta, 17

Zilker, Andrew, 46–47
Zilker, Charles, 46–47
Zilker Park, 47
Zodiac, 113, 114